TREES IN TOWNS

TREES IN TOWNS

Maintenance and management

Editors
Brian Clouston
Kathy Stansfield

Contributors
Giles Biddle, Peter Bridgeman, David Burdekin,
David Harte, Alex Novell, Chris Wild

The Architectural Press: London

'The tradesman, the attorney, comes out of the din and the craft of the streets and sees the sky and the woods, and is a man again. In the eternal calm, he finds himself.'

Ralph Waldo Emerson, *Nature,* 1836

The drawings in chapters 1, 3 and 5 are by Clive McWilliam

First published in 1981 by the Architectural Press Ltd, London

© Brian Clouston 1981

ISBN 0 85139 658 5

Printed in Great Britain by
Mackays of Chatham, Kent

Contents

Notes on contributors

Brian Clouston is senior partner and founder of one of the largest landscape design firms in Europe. He is currently Senior Vice President of the Landscape Institute and has edited several books including *Landscape Design with Plants, After the Elm,* and *Landscape by Design.*

Kathy Stansfield is a writer/editor on planning, landscape and the environment for *The Architects' Journal.* She has worked as researcher, co-editor and contributor on books such as *Landscape Design with Plants, After the Elm* and *Pioneers in British Planning.*

Giles Biddle is senior partner and founder of a firm of arboricultural consultants, Tree Conservation Ltd. He serves on the Standing Committee on Arboricultural Education, on the Forestry Training Council, and is chairman-elect of the Arboricultural Association.

Peter Bridgeman was Head of the Arboricultural Department at Merrist Wood Agricultural College for nine years, and is now head of his own consultancy, Peter Bridgeman and Associates.

David Burdekin is Principal Pathologist at the Forest Research Station in Farnham, Surrey. He advises both local authorities and individuals with an interest in trees and tree diseases.

David Harte is Lecturer in Law at the University of Newcastle-upon-Tyne; he also teaches students in planning and landscape architecture in the Department of Town and Country Planning.

Alex Novell is a director of Brian Clouston and Partners, and has previously worked in both private practice and local authorities.

Christopher Wild died while this book was in preparation. He had worked on a wide range of industrial landscape projects both in private practice and local government.

1

The tree and the city

Brian Clouston and Alex Novell

Of all the elements in our landscape, surely the tree has the greatest capacity to bring the presence of nature into the built environment (see Plates 1 to 17). Even a single mature tree can soften the uncompromising angular shapes of modern buildings, or disguise the all too familiar, unhappy juxtaposition of vernacular and contemporary architecture.

Yet the presence of trees in our towns is often accidental and taken for granted. Care and thought are required to ensure a tree's survival in a hostile environment, qualities which are often lacking as trees continue to be cut down or mutilated where they are seen to be a nuisance. Where large tracts of parkland give our cities character and greenery these are much more often the result of former country estates having been engulfed by development than a conscious inclusion in the design for urban growth. In those areas associated with the growth of industry, and in many of our inner city areas, trees in the urban environment are still a rarity. Even in those few hallowed areas where men of forethought and vision have provided a rich natural canopy, many trees are already past maturity and few are being replaced. Dutch elm disease and the drought of the mid-1970s have decimated the tree population of some suburbs and town parks, and planting on a large scale is needed to replace it. If not, it will be too late for the next generation to enjoy the beauty and real benefits of trees in towns. New trees must be seen as our investment for the future.

THE EXAMPLE OF THE PAST

Not until the eighteenth century could trees be considered a part of the urban environment in any conscious way. The growing interest and creativity in the arts, architecture and landscape meant that wealthy patrons were prepared to spend large sums of money on buildings and gardens. The seeds of the eighteenth-century landscape movement, which was to green at least the more affluent parts of the town, were sown in Britain's country estates, where the inspiration of poet and painter was translated into reality through architecture and landscape design.

Consult the Genius of the Place in all;
That tells the Waters or to rise, or fall;
Or helps th'ambitious Hill the heavens to scale,
Or scoops in arching theatres the Vale;
Calls in the Country, catches op'ning glades,
Joins willing woods, and varies shades from shades;
Now breaks, or now directs, th'intending lines;
Paint as you plant, and as you work, design.

Alexander Pope

The work of Capability Brown, William Kent and others emphasised natural beauty and, in so doing, departed from formal garden traditions. Almost for the first time, the visual qualities of trees became important. Brown used the rounded forms of native beech, plane, lime and chestnut to complement gently flowing land form in a harmonious composition. Kent 'composed with the eye of a painter', using a palate of grass and trees. Balance in composition, depth and harmony of colour, and sensitivity to light and shade were as much a part of his landscape design as they would have been on a painter's canvas. The Reverend William Gilpin used the sinewy forms of ash, oak, elm, birch, cedar and pine in creating his ideal of the Picturesque – that which was not merely beautiful but which embodied all the qualities of nature.

In our towns, the tradition of planting trees along streets owes much to the layout of French Baroque gardens, epitomised by Versailles (1661-74) with its long, straight avenues. It was a style easily adapted to street design, notably in L'Enfant's plan for Washington D.C. in 1791 and, later, in Haussman's designs for Paris. These cities are characterised by tree-lined straight avenues and open spaces and, in their turn, they inspired the plans of American cities in the early twentieth century.

These two streams of influence, the English Romantic landscape and the French Baroque garden, were together responsible for the green appearance of the wealthier parts of our cities. The Romantic influence is most noticeable in parks and suburbs extending into the previously well-wooded commons and estates, while the French Baroque is more evident in our central areas, adding importance to high-class residential areas and public places. The squares and streets of London's West End, built in the early 1800s, were lined with trees and formed private open space for wealthy middle-class housing. The original evergreens such as yew and fir were later replaced with plane trees and sycamores, better suited to the urban scene and more resistant to pollution. Now, of course, the squares and Royal Parks of London make a unique contribution to the city's public open space. As towns expanded, the villa and its garden became the status symbols of the growing middle class. Popularising the fashions of the wealthy, there was a constant reduction in the scale of the 'private estate' to fit the increasingly wide-ranging size of plot and pocket.

But these developments were for private enjoyment only. Awareness of the need for trees and green spaces for public use grew out of the reaction to poor urban conditions and over-crowding and, during the latter half of the nineteenth century, urban parks were created in a number of large towns.

Parks

During the nineteenth century, landscape designers and gardeners in England moved away from the natural forms, which had been exploited so sympathetically during the previous century, to a much more academic interest in botany and horticulture. It was a time of experimentation with a much broader palette of plants, many imported from other temperate regions and developed in a bewildering variety by the expanding industry of the horticultural and plant nurseries. The nineteenth century gardenesque style of landscape design is viewed by many as a debasement of earlier traditions. Gardens and parks were seen as places for displaying individual trees and plants. John Loudon and, later, Joseph Paxton developed park designs, using beds of mixed species separated by lawns set with ornamental trees. Parks were places to walk through, to sit in and admire, an escape from urban surroundings. They were cut off from the town by a fence or wall, and locked at night.

The first public park to secure land by act of Parliament was at Birkenhead, Liverpool, begun in 1844 and designed by Joseph Paxton. London had always been well endowed with Royal Parks but these were not generally open to the public

3

and, like the smaller open spaces, were mainly concentrated in the West End. From the latter half of the nineteenth century, public parks were created in slow response to public demand, the first being Victoria Park in the East End, in 1841. Countrywide the process was unco-ordinated and piecemeal. Nevertheless, it provided the stimulus for park development in Europe and America. Paris, like London, had open spaces owned by the crown: the Tuileries and the Champs-Elysées, and other gardens, were open for public use in the early 1800s. Later, parks created as part of Eugène Haussmann's transformation of Paris between 1852 and 1869 took the English romantic landscape and later gardenesque tradition as a model. In addition, great tree-lined boulevards were created in the city, echoing those at Versailles, as much for military as aesthetic effect, and smaller open spaces were modelled on London's squares.

In Germany, disused town fortifications provided space for public promenades and gardens, and provision of tree-planted green spaces was a characteristic of many German towns in the nineteenth century, notably Magdeburg, Frankfurt, Berlin and Hamburg.

In America, recognition of the need for open space can be traced back to the 1830s, when new burial grounds were set in attractively landscaped surroundings at the edge of town, partly for reasons of hygiene. They proved so popular that they stimulated the creation of public parks in which the English influence was noticeable. This was also true of the leafy suburbs of American towns. The landscape architect, A.J. Downing, was responsible for many of these schemes, his influence in America paralleling that of Loudon in England, with whose work he was familiar. His Llewellyn Park in New Jersey, started in 1852, was similar in concept to Ebenezer Howard's Garden City idea, first publicised in England in 1898. He was largely responsible for the planting of trees along streets which became popular in many American towns. One of the first major parks in American cities was New York's Central Park, designed by Olmstead and Vaux and started in 1858. A lake was created and the effect of existing tree-covered slopes enhanced by mass planting which screened the buildings of the surrounding city from view. It was a huge popular and financial success, despite the fact that it occupied approximately 300 hectares of prime urban land. Local property values increased enormously, and the example was followed by many American cities. Most notable in terms of concept, however, was Olmstead's park plan for Boston. Green spaces formed a linked system throughout the city, connected by tree-lined parkways. It eventually became part of a regional open space network, including areas of marsh, wood, river and beach. This went far beyond the English view of the park contained within a fence and has much more in common with recent trends in city planning. Its example spread in America and back to Europe, where it has inspired developments in Holland, Germany and Scandinavia.

In England, reaction against the industrial city produced reform movements which took up the need for contact with nature on grounds of public health and the morality of the working classes. The company towns of Bourneville and Port Sunlight in the late nineteenth century were heavily planted with trees in streets and gardens. So were the garden cities advocated by Howard and built at Letchworth and Welwyn, now richly green towns with remarkable numbers of trees. But these were isolated examples. Towns expanded rapidly, more houses had gardens, and trees from old estates and farmland sometimes survived to become part of the urban sprawl. There was no overall thought given to landscaping and tree-planting, and trees were readily sacrificed to building and road-widening schemes. The park remained secure within its fence, although the formal Victorian designs gave way to freer landscapes displaying carefully worked out displays of native and exotic species, epitomised by the work of William Robinson and Gertrude Jekyll. They created gardens of great beauty, but this tradition, though impressive, lacked application at city scale and brought with it enormous requirements for specialised knowledge and after-care.

In Europe, the American example had more impact. The penetration of the city by greenery was advocated in Germany in 1924 by Fritz Schumacher, Hamburg's director of building, as the 'great breathing space of the town'. The city already had a huge central park with a large lake designed for a variety of sports and other activities, its simple planting design including large areas of trees.

In Scandinavia, Denmark developed numerous city parks, notably the 400-acre West Forest Park in Copenhagen, and, in Sweden, where nature had always been a much more accepted part of the city, interlinked systems of open space evolved naturally out of the landscape tradition. The Finnish new town

5

of Tapiola even gave trees as much importance as housing and roads. Holland's Bos Park in Amsterdam is one of the best-known examples of an extensive city park. Started in 1931, the 900-hectare park has 400 hectares of woodland and 160 hectares of water. The contrast between tree, meadow and water on reclaimed polder land creates interest in a landscape where hills and valleys are absent. The choice of planting relies on indigenous vegetation rather than exotics – oak, beech, linden, birch, ash, maple, poplar, alder and willow being the main species. Often, the establishment of woodland is seen as a two-stage process. First, poplar, willow, birch and alder are planted as pioneer species, and these are underplanted with woodland shrubs. Growth, as a result, has been vigorous and disease-free. creating a sheltered environment in which larger-growing forest trees, like oak and beech, can thrive. The main entrance of the park is only $3\frac{1}{2}$ miles from central Amsterdam and up to 100,000 people a day use the park. It owes its undoubted success to the woodland character offered by this type of planting, rather than to any grand concepts of design. The Bos Park has started a tradition in Holland which is still developing. Dutch experiments designed to free the landscape from 'uniformity and monotony' and 'to restore the rich diversity of the natural, cultural land-scape', are now opening up new frontiers in planning the urban environment. During the past 20 years, a number of schemes relating ecologically based landscape design and new housing schemes have been carried out. At the Bijlmermeer, Amsterdam, the inhuman scale of 8-storey tower blocks was much reduced by mass planting of woodland and carefully planted communal courts, moving away from the idea of the private garden. Further schemes have developed the relationship between planting and children's play. The idea of introducing children to nature through the sympathetic use and siting of trees in play areas has been pioneered in towns like Delft in Holland and quickly taken up in Germany, Sweden and Switzerland. Other schemes have worked towards creating biological diversity in plant life. Notable are the Heem nature parks at Amstelveen created by Landwehr, where over 500 species of trees, shrubs and herbs have been used, in response to difficult ground conditions, where the underlying peat could not support forest-sized trees alone (Ruff).

Urban woodlands

The last few years have seen a movement in England away from the loose, large-scale spaces characteristic of some of our new towns and motorways, dubbed 'prairie planning', and essentially still a palette of manicured trees and grass in a land form of gently swelling, man-created mounds. It is a movement to bring nature right into our cities by the creation of urban woodlands, following continental examples in Holland and Germany, and also those in the United States. The urban woodland, like its country counterpart, contains the varied plants and associated wildlife, much richer than that of the usual, more specialised, less dense tree-planting, with all the advantages this has in ecological terms. Smaller clumps of trees or copses are increasingly being linked to other woods by paths, disused railway tracks, canal banks, major road corridors or other linear green spaces, to form a network. London has its fair share of existing woodlands which have long been part of the city, notably in Hampstead, Richmond and Wimbledon, and some of the New Towns such as Cumbernauld and Peterlee have incorporated existing woodlands. But we have a long way to go before we can compare with towns in Holland, Germany and Scandinavia, where the feeling is rather that the town has been carved out of the forest than that the forest has been added to the town.

Examples in Britain do exist, but they are few and far between. In Cumbernauld, 400 hectares of woodland were planted at an early stage in the town's development. This is much larger than the area which can be afforded in older towns in more heavily populated areas. In Stoke-on-Trent, Hanley Forest Park covers 40 hectares of reclaimed land, rare in its emphasis on trees. At Catterick Garrison, in Yorkshire, large tracts of derelict and disused land have been afforested, combining with existing woodland to create a landscape framework capable of absorbing the many and varied land-uses of an army town. It may be that tree-planting is the best use for some of our contaminated urban wastelands which may be unfit or unready for development. Slowly the idea of large- and small-scale tree-planting is gaining acceptance and the idea of the urban park is diffusing into a network of open spaces, even in our older towns. In Manchester, for example, derelict industrial river valleys which penetrate the town are being planted with trees and large urban parks have been proposed for the inner city areas of

Glasgow, London and Liverpool. A garden city may take root in such an area, in which the emphasis would be very much on woodland planting and nature conservation.

It is perhaps ironic that our attitude to nature has returned almost full circle to the concept of the Picturesque held by Richard Payne Knight and the Reverend William Gilpin in England's eighteenth-century Romantic landscape movement. Nature should not only look beautiful, but should embody all the variety, ecological diversity and continuity of life itself. A single tree can act as a foil to urban architecture and serve to remind us of the countryside, but how much better to accept nature as the living, breathing part of our urban fabric, to provide a refuge not only for us, but for the vast range of other creatures which give us so much pleasure.

It remains to be seen what actually happens. The success of any planting scheme relies on much more than soundness of concept. A solid appreciation of design factors, choice of species, woodland ecology and management are all of crucial importance. It is hoped that a discussion of these and other topics later in the book will at least open the reader's eyes to the possibilities of further increased use of trees in towns.

TREES IN DESIGN

Whether used singly as specimens, in groups and clumps, or as belts of woodland, trees provide changing year-round interest – the texture and patterns of leaves, bark and bare branches, the seasonal change of leaf-colour, and the appearance of blossom, fruit and seed. A single tree can become the focal point of a courtyard or small urban space, or break the line of buildings in a street. The sculptural qualities of trees used in this way can be enhanced by night illumination, casting shadows on surrounding buildings, paving or grass.

Trees can be used in built-up areas to direct movement, clarifying the use of spaces and the purpose of buildings, screening service areas and car parks, and emphasising and locating entrances and stressing their relative importance. They lend shelter and shade, and make outdoor space more attractive for sitting or play. In visual terms, they can be used to frame views, softening the hard outlines of buildings and roads, and adding interest to the townscape. Trees can heighten the sense of enclosure and perspective, creating the impression of more or

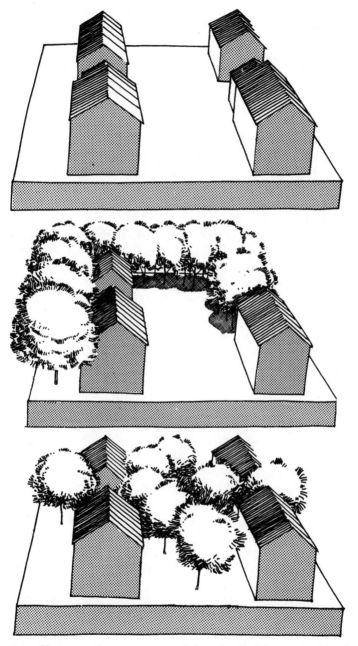

Fig. 1.1. Treatment of space: **a** *untreated;* **b** *scale of buildings reduced by planting to emphasise the space,* **c** *scale of space itself broken up by planting*

less space, as desired (figure **1.1**). This can be reinforced by colour. Blues and greys recede, yellows and reds advance. In this way, trees make spaces easier to comprehend, dividing large areas into a series of smaller spaces.

Spacing and pattern can be varied, uneven numbers for an irregular, natural effect, even numbers, such as a pair on each side of an entrance, or an avenue, where a formal effect is desired. Informality in planting design is generally more sympathetic to the tree as a living, changing organism. The use of a variety of species also has the advantage of avoiding devastating losses, such as those from Dutch elm disease. Meanness in tree planting is a false economy. The desired effect is much more likely to be achieved by generous planting initially, thinned out as required. Trees benefit from close planting, providing shelter as they grow. Often the laborious and costly planting of semi-mature trees in an attempt to produce instant effect ends in disappointment when growth is severely retarded. It may even kill the tree. A group of younger, more vigorous trees, planted together, will adjust more rapidly to the urban conditions and ultimately provide much more impact.

Advance planting
There is much to be said for the creation of woodlands and structure planting as unifying elements in the town. In New Towns, advantage could be taken of existing woodlands to achieve such effects. It is much more difficult in existing towns, but areas of derelict inner urban land and waste urban fringe which have lain idle for years, awaiting development, could be temporarily planted at little cost, thereby much improving the local environment. There would then be scope for creating green spaces, with trees already well grown, when the land is finally developed – 'painting with an axe' the Dutch parks director, Jan Guldemond, called it. This land would require careful analysis of site conditions, soil and micro-climate, and selection of quick-growing species, (pioneer species in difficult conditions) with slower-growing trees amongst them for a more long-term effect. This would go some way to reversing the more common process whereby planting is only taken into consideration at a later stage of the design, when building layouts have been decided. The best results come from working with nature, giving trees the best possible chance of survival and reducing many of the well-meant but fruitless efforts which fail through lack of understanding.

Tree benefits

The planned inclusion of trees in towns was seen in the nineteenth century as beneficial to the health and morality of the working classes, as recorded in the report of the 1843 Select Committee on the Health of Towns. A year later, the New York Board of Health defined trees as improvers of city air and encouraged the planting of them in built areas. They were, of course, appreciated for their visual qualities, and of benefit to builders and ratepayers as enhancing property values.

Values have changed. Concern for morality and health has given way to concern for nature itself as an all-embracing context for human life, susceptible to unthinking exploitation. And research has indicated benefits of a surprisingly tangible kind, which can be shown to go a long way towards improving living conditions in our towns.

Environmental factors

Climate
Every area has its own particular micro-climate and, often, the climatic effects of wind, rain and solar radiation are intensified by the built environment. The judicious use of plants can improve human comfort in urban conditions, provided careful thought is given to the types of plants, their location and after-care, to give them the best possible chance of survival in what is, after all, an unnatural environment.

Solar radiation, that is, direct or reflected sunlight, can be

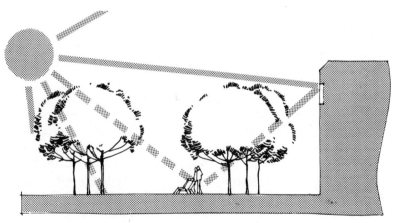

Fig. 1.2. Solar-radiation effects reduced by planting

11

moderated by planting which reflects less radiation than most smooth man-made surfaces (figure **1.2**). The darker the plant, the more effective it will be, and conifers are particularly useful in this way. But even trees of light foliage, like birch, rowan, willow and poplar, will reduce light-levels by about 50 per cent, while denser, heavier trees such as horse-chestnut, plane, maple and beech may cut out more than 90 per cent of the available light (Robinette). In winter, deciduous trees allow the available light and warmth through their leafless crowns, an important benefit in temperate regions.

Temperature control
In artificial conditions, temperature differences are often extreme, summer heat being reflected from buildings or cold air funnelled between them. Trees can reduce the daily temperature fluctuation by creating shade and absorbing excessive radiation, by trapping warm air in their canopies at night and by sheltering the area from cold winds. Dense evergreen planting close to a wall can prevent heat loss from buildings, saving around 30 per cent of energy loss from a house with a temperature of 70° (Robinette); though caution must be exercised in the selection and planting of trees to avoid root problems and excessive loss of daylight.

Wind and shelter
Strong wind currents are often formed in the urban environment where tall buildings create eddies and funnel the wind along streets and narrow passageways. The effects can be greatly reduced by planting strong shelter-belts (figure **1.3**). Trees will decrease turbulence more effectively than solid screens like walls and fencing. The effectiveness of tree-planting will depend on the species, and the height and the width of the barrier. The looser the foliage, the greater the protection behind it. American studies have shown that wind speeds on the leeward side of a dense barrier of spruce or fir can be cut by 15 to 20 per cent but the looser textured Lombardy poplar gives 60 per cent reduction (Robinette). The wind will be controlled for up to 5 times the height of the barrier to windward, and for 10 to 15 times the height to leeward. The taller the trees, the more rows will need to be planted, unless the barrier is reinforced with thick underplanting, but a barrier 15 to 20 metres wide has a significant impact.

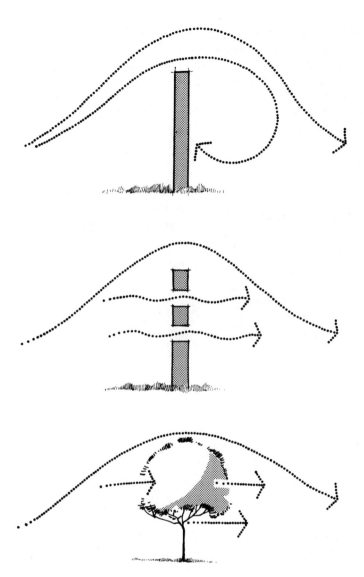

Fig. 1.3. Wind effects using different types of barrier: **a** *solid;* **b** *wind-break;* **c** *tree*

With careful analysis of site conditions and seasonal variations, belts of trees can be planted to provide shelter from pre-
vailing winds and to deflect the wind from another direction.
Native species for shelter-belts are more likely to blend into the

local landscape, and using a limited number of species enables the character of the tree to be fully exploited. In a broader sense, belts of woodland can act as green lungs allowing cool, clean air from the surrounding countryside to penetrate and circulate within the city, as in schemes for tree-planting in the derelict valleys which penetrate Manchester.

Noise
Traffic is one of the worst sources of noise in urban areas. Research in Germany and America indicates that plants can screen disturbing sound-levels by absorbing the sound through foliage or deflecting it through branches and from tree trunks (figure **1.4**). The effectiveness is unpredictable, depending on the

Fig. 1.4. Noise buffer formed by planting and earth mound between the road and houses

nature of the sound, wind direction, time of year, and the species, amount and density of planting. Sound-levels can be reduced by as much as 7 decibels per 100 feet width of planting. Soft surfaces absorb more sound than hard ones, so planting in built-up areas helps offset some of the problems, though, in winter, much of the effect is lost if the trees are deciduous. A combination of tall trees and shrubs 25 to 35 feet wide has been found to be effective in controlling highway noise, though this can be much improved when planting is combined with earth buffers (Robinette)

Air pollution
Despite legislation to try to control air-pollution and noise-levels, these are still often greater than desirable, and controls may vary from country to country. In Frankfurt, Germany, dust-levels were found to be three or four times greater in treeless streets than in tree-lined streets. The air is cleaned by the effect of photosynthesis, where the polluting agent is diluted with

oxygen-rich air. Dirt, dust, smoke, pollen and chemicals are held by the leaves – very noticeable near quarry workings where the foliage is often coated with deposits – and either absorbed or washed off by rain. See figure **1.5**.

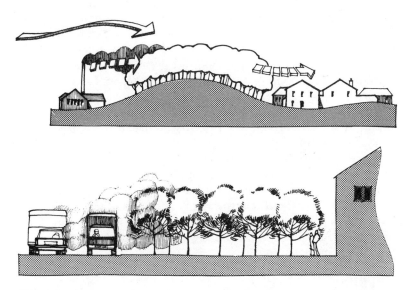

Fig. 1.5. Removal of air pollution: **a** *polluted air from factory filtered through planting;* **b** *dust-laden air from road filtered by street planting*

Parks and tree-filled spaces in Stuttgart have reduced air-pollution to a significant degree by allowing clean air from the surrounding countryside to penetrate the town.

Soil conservation
Urban soils tend to be dry, shallow and poor, and particularly prone to erosion where exposed to the effects of wind and rain. Trees provide protection by binding the soil with their roots and improve it by humus and leaf litter. The tree canopy protects the soil surface from direct sunlight and heavy rain. Soil moisture-content is controlled by trees taking up water through their roots for transpiration and reducing water movement, and by their drainage requirements. Trees can also help to drain areas of hard paving if channels can be designed to take surface water to planted areas.

15

Wildlife

The ecological importance of wildlife in our towns is now recognised and can be encouraged through interlinked planted spaces. Traditional parks and areas of carefully mown grass and trees do not provide sufficiently varied and safe habitats for a wide range of flora and fauna, and do little to restore the ecological balance. Planting of native species, particularly in urban woodlands, provides much greater opportunities for reintroducing wildlife into the heart of our urban areas. The greater the 'edge' between woodlands and open or built land, the richer and more diverse the wildlife will be.

It can be seen that the tree is the only natural element in our surroundings of sufficient scale and power to reduce the excesses of our hard artificial environment to a balanced harmony of architecture and nature. Without trees, our cities are barren wastes of concrete and stone, tarmac and sterile grassland. Trees add life. But, without a massive effort on our part to recognise their many benefits and consciously plant and maintain them, the sight of majestic, mature trees in our great cities is likely to be a thing of the past.

REFERENCES

1 T. Aldous (ed), *Trees and buildings: complement or conflict...*, London, RIBA and Tree Council, Conference papers, 1979
2 G.F. Chadwick, *The park and the town*, London, Architectural Press, 1966
3 J.B. Clouston (ed), *Landscape design with plants*, London, Heinemann, 1977
4 H. Johnson, *The international book of trees*, first published 1973, London, Mitchell Beazley, 1977
5 I.L. Laurie (ed), *Nature in cities*, New York, John Wiley, 1979
6 G.O. Robinette, *Plants, people and environmental quality*, Washington DC, US Department of the Interior National Parks Service, 1972
7 A.R. Ruff, *Holland and the ecological landscape*, Manchester, University Department of Town and Country Planning, 1979
8 Town and Country Planning Association, *An outline prospectus for a third garden city*, London, TCPA, 1979

2

Physical problems caused by trees to buildings and services

Giles Biddle

Trees are the largest physical objects, apart from buildings, in the urban environment, mature trees being higher and occupying more space than domestic housing. It is not surprising, therefore, that these two objects come into frequent conflict for the available space. It is necessary for the arboriculturist and landscape architect to appreciate and help to resolve this conflict, so as to produce an environment which benefits from the advantages provided by trees without their causing undue social aggravation. Perhaps one of the most commonly heard cries is 'I like trees, but not in front of my house'. Universal adoption of such an attitude would result in relegating all trees to isolated public open spaces, and destroying the ameliorating effect of trees on the often monotonous and harsh outlines of urban housing.

The conflict between trees and buildings can take many forms. In extreme cases, the trunk or branches may break and cause direct physical damage but, more commonly, there can be complaints about obstruction of light, blockage of gutters from falling leaves or fruit, or unsightly secretions (honeydew drip) from trees. Trees can also damage overhead telephone or powerlines, and even interfere with television reception.

These above-ground effects of the tree are comparatively obvious and easy to appreciate, but the underground conflict can frequently be even more serious. Roots can block drains and damage paths, walls and buildings by their direct growth. Even more important can be the problems associated with tree roots causing changes in moisture content of shrinkable clay soils, resulting in foundation movement and structural damage to buildings. These problems have been particularly highlighted by periods of drought in recent years (1947 and 1975/76), and this has led to widespread pressure to separate trees and buildings to distances which landscape architects and environmentalists

17

would find wholly unacceptable.

This chapter outlines these problems, with particular emphasis on problems of damage on clay soils, and suggests ways of resolving these conflicts.

ABOVE-GROUND PROBLEMS ASSOCIATED WITH TREES

The aerial parts of a tree are obvious, the problems which they cause can be readily appreciated, and this makes it easier to reach a compromise between these problems and the aesthetic benefits conferred by the tree. However, this does not prevent the attitude of 'I like trees but not in front of my house' and it is, therefore, relevant to consider the problems which the trees cause.

Obstruction of light

Branches growing in front of, or above, a window can block lateral or vertical light falling on that window. The amount of obstruction will depend on the proximity of the branches, and the density of the foliage. Where this obstruction is to living rooms, it can cause serious inconvenience to the inhabitants, possibly necessitating the use of artificial lights during the day.

The obvious solution to the problem is to keep sufficient distance between the tree and window, either by planting at sufficient distance or by pruning off offending branches. Sometimes it can be sufficient to remove only the lower branches of a tree which overhang a house: this crown-lifting can permit sufficient lateral light to reach the windows beneath the main canopy.

Where the branches belong to a tree in the ownership of the inhabitant, such pruning causes no difficulty, provided the trees are not the subject of a Tree Preservation Order. Similarly, if the trees grow on adjacent land but have branches overhanging, these can be pruned back to the boundary and this will usually permit sufficient light. However, situations can arise where the windows are so close to the boundary that the trees on the far side can still cause significant loss of light. The legal remedy in this situation depends on whether there is an easement to 'right of light'. Such right can be established if the window has enjoyed 20 years of uninterrupted light, in which case the owners of the tree can be required to prune or fell the tree so as to maintain this right to light coming from a lateral direction.

18

Blocking of gutters

This is a regular problem occurring every autumn. The risks depend on the proximity of the branches to the gutter, the shape of gutter and overhanging roof, and the size and type of leaf. Large soft leaves, such as sycamore, can cause particular problems. Some relief can be obtained by placing a wire mesh over the gutter so as to prevent the leaves collecting in a soggy mess and washing into the downpipes.

Physical impact

Intact branches striking a building can easily be dealt with by suitable pruning to maintain adequate clearance.

Damage from falling trees or branches can only be prevented by recognition of the dangerous branch or tree before the accident. Many legal cases have clearly established that a tree owner can only be held liable for such accident if he could reasonably have appreciated the potentially dangerous condition of the tree or branch. This normally means that it must show some significant defect, such as fungal growths, a cavity of sufficient size to weaken the tree, thinness of the foliage indicative of decay of the roots, dead wood, etc.

However, it must also be appreciated that, even if a tree shows no significant defect and there is no justification in thinking that it might be dangerous, a person living close to the tree may still be concerned. In some cases, this concern can lead to great personal stress, with people living in fear whenever there are gales. In such situations, reassurance about the safety of the tree can be meaningless, as no tree can be guaranteed 100 per cent safe. These social attitudes must always be considered when deciding on the suitability of trees in the vicinity of housing.

Interference with overhead cables.

Statutory undertakers, such as electricity boards and the Post Office, have a right to prune trees to maintain adequate clearance for overhead cables. In this country, this usually only entails regular cutting back, but the American Utility Companies are increasingly turning to growth-retardant chemicals to control tree shape and re-growth. This can either take the form of hormones (such as indole-acetic acid) incorporated in bitumastic tree paints to restrict re-growth, or application of growth inhibitors, such as maleic hydrazide, by foliar spray or trunk injection.

Interference with television reception

The Department of Environment Arboricultural Advisory and Information Service Research Note 14, 1979, describes the serious effect that trees can sometimes have on television reception. The greatest effects tend to occur in the higher frequencies of the UHF band, which are covered by channels 39 to 68. The trees can obstruct or deflect the transmission, causing shadows where reception is difficult. The worst effects come from evergreen trees, particularly conifers, and during wet weather the effects are further enhanced. There is much less effect from deciduous trees when they are bare in winter. Further problems can arise when the signal is reflected so as to arrive appreciably later than the direct signal, giving rise to a delayed image or 'ghost' on the screen. This effect can vary if the trees are moving in the wind.

The problems are unimportant in strong signal areas and, where signals are weak, it can be overcome by mounting the aerial above the tree tops. This can obviously be difficult with tall trees and, in this situation, it may be necessary to use a high-gain aerial, possibly with a masthead amplifier. High-gain aerials can also reduce the problems of ghosting, as they are highly directional and can cut out the reflected signal.

UNDERGROUND PROBLEMS ASSOCIATED WITH TREES

Blocking of drains

The roots of trees which manage to penetrate a drain are liable to proliferate and produce an extensive system within the drain (Plate **16**). This can lead to blocking of the drain, particularly in the case of foul-water drains which are carrying solids. The problems usually start because of an existing crack in the drain. This can produce a local supply of water and, if there are any roots in the vicinity, they will exploit this water. If the crack is large enough for a fine root to enter the drain, it will usually find that the drain provides the ideal conditions of water and air for root growth. A single root entering the drain can branch repeatedly to produce an extensive system capable of causing a blockage. Furthermore, the radial growth of the root where it penetrates the drain may exert adequate force to enlarge the crack, thus aggravating the leak and allowing more roots to enter.

It is rare for a root to be able to break an intact drain. This is only likely to occur where the drain is very close to the main trunk of the tree and the direct radial growth of the large anchor roots exerts sufficient local pressure to cause cracking. Alternatively, drains may be cracked by soil movements associated with clay shrinkage caused by the drying of the soil by the tree roots. These problems can be avoided by correct construction, using flexible-jointed drains.

The identification of roots by the Royal Botanic Gardens at Kew, has included remarkably few root samples originating from drains (Richardson – personal communication). Of 22 samples, 9 were from the *Salicaceae* (willows and poplar), 4 from *Acer* (which includes sycamore), 3 from *Prunus* (cherry), and one each from plane, birch, horse chestnut, oak, elm and apple. These results confirm my personal observation that the problems are most commonly caused by willow and sycamore.

Roots can be removed by cleaning with rods, but the broken ends left in the drain are always liable to re-grow. Where permissible, a more satisfactory method is to try to kill off the roots with a herbicide, which will be translocated back so as to kill the length of root which has penetrated the drain. This can be achieved by passing a spray nozzle down the drain, and applying a herbicide such as 2,4,5-T and leaving sufficient time for the herbicide to be absorbed before flushing. Alternatively, the drain can be blocked at the lower end, and a dilute solution of a material such as metham sodium used to fill the drain and kill the root.

Damage by physical growth of roots
Damage by growth of roots must be carefully distinguished from the much more serious problems associated with roots causing drying and shrinkage of a clay soil. Problems from the direct growth of roots are caused by their increasing diameter. It is thus mainly a problem in the immediate vicinity of the trunk of the tree, where there are large anchor roots and also the large mass of the base of the tree.

The forces exerted by this radial growth are comparatively small. The root will be distorted if it encounters any substantial object, and the root will either fail to expand, or deform in the opposite direction into the adjacent soil.

However, where the objects resisting the growth exert insufficient force, they are liable to be lifted or pushed aside. This most frequently affects paving slabs which can be lifted by roots running just beneath the surface. Large roots can also lift and crack lightly loaded walls such as low boundary walls (Plate **20**) or cause cracking of driveways. The radial growth of the base of a tree can be sufficient to push boundary walls sideways, and even house walls can be damaged but only if they are very close to the tree. Problems of this type are usually restricted to structures within a distance not greater than the circumference of the trunk.

The problems can usually be avoided by severing the offending roots and, provided this only entails a few surface roots, it will affect neither the stability nor health of the tree. If necessary, the root which is lifting a wall can be bridged.

Damage of this type is normally comparatively minor, and develops slowly as the roots or trunk grow. Despite this, it gives rise to many complaints that the trees are causing damage, and concern that such damage may spread to the main structure of the house. This damage is sometimes used as justification for legal claims and an injunction that a tree should be removed. Whilst such damage may be the subject of an indemnity claim against a third-party owner of a tree, it is dubious whether an injunction to restrain the commission of further damage would be successful. The case in the Court of Appeal, *Miller* v. *Jackson* (1977) 1QB 966, held by a majority that, since the grant of an injunction involved the exercise of an equitable jurisdiction, the Court was empowered and under a duty to weigh the balance between public and private interest.

As the public interests derive benefit from the aesthetic advantage of trees in an urban situation, they should not lightly be deprived of such advantage to prevent damage to boundary walls or similar structures which are of a lower order of importance and which do not directly affect the structure of the house.

Damage resulting from clay shrinkage

The greatest and most serious conflict between trees and buildings occurs on shrinkable clay soils. These soils suffer from dimensional changes with change in moisture content, shrinking as they dry and swelling when they rehydrate. The amount of drying, and thus shrinkage, can be greatly increased by the removal of water from the soil by tree roots. If this occurs in the soil beneath the foundations of a building, when the clay shrinks, the foundations subside and this can cause structural damage to the whole fabric of the building.

It must be emphasised that the roots themselves are not involved in this damage. It is only by their action of removing

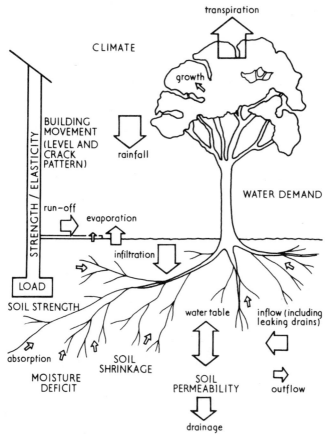

Fig. 2.1. Diagram (not to scale) showing main water movements (lower-case) and factors for consideration when investigating possible involvement of trees or cause of subsidence damage (from Biddle[1])

water that damage can result under certain circumstances. The essential feature in the system is change in the water (i.e. moisture content) of the soil. The importance of water is illustrated in figure **2.1.** which shows the various factors which influence the balance of water in the system. Water enters the system as rainfall and, to a lesser extent, as inflow from surrounding ground or from leaking drains and, during the winter, by a rise in the water table. In the absence of vegetation, water is lost by evaporation or run-off from the soil surface, and by lateral or vertical drainage. In open ground or under grass, there will be a seasonal cycle of loss of moisture during the summer months when evaporation exceeds rainfall, followed by increasing moisture content in the winter. However, evaporation losses only affect the surface layers of soil, and will not normally cause any changes below a depth of one metre.

If a building is introduced to the system, it will interfere with this balance by excluding rainfall from the area beneath the building and by preventing evaporation. The effect of a building is therefore to reduce the normal seasonal cycle, and the soil moisture content beneath the foundations remains in equilibrium.

Introduce a tree, and the balance can be seriously affected. During the summer, when the tree is in leaf, it is losing water as transpiration, to an extent far exceeding the evaporation losses from the soil surface and the transpiration from grass. This water demand must be satisfied by the extraction of moisture from the soil during the summer. With soils of high permeability (e.g. sand), the rates of lateral water movement can be very rapid, so that the whole soil dries fairly uniformly and there is a progressive lowering of the water table. However, with impermeable soils such as heavy clay, a localised deficit develops in the rooting zone and, if the roots are exploiting the soil beneath the foundations, this soil will become desiccated. During winter months, when transpiration losses from the tree cease, the water deficits may be corrected, provided the soil is sufficiently permeable. In this situation, the effect of the root activity is to increase only the normal seasonal fluctuation in moisture content but, with soils of very low permeability, the water deficit may not be corrected during a single winter, and it may increase progressively as a tree grows and increases its water demand. These permanent water deficits in the rooting zone are a feature of the heavy impermeable clay soils.

Changes in moisture content can produce dimensional changes in clay soils, but the amount of this is very dependent on the type of clay. Factors of particular relevance are the clay mineralogy, particle size distribution, and percentage composition of non-shrinkable sand or silt. It is therefore essential to consider the characteristics of the clay when assessing the amounts of shrinkage which may occur.

Other characteristics of the clay are also of relevance. Pressure, such as that exerted by the foundation load, will cause a clay to consolidate, while excessive loading can lead to complete failure.

Uniform movements of the foundations do not produce damage, but differential movements will stress a building and, ultimately, produce cracking. The design of the building can influence the amount of differential movement, with structures such as bay windows being particularly vulnerable, and differential foundation depths seriously aggravating the risks of damage. The method of construction can also be important, as the lime mortar used in older buildings tended to be far more flexible than modern cement joints and this permitted the building to distort without cracking.

It can thus be appreciated that there are many factors to consider when assessing the risks of a tree causing foundation damage. These may be summarised as:

a) rooting pattern of the tree
b) the pattern of moisture deficit produced by the roots
c) the extent of soil shrinkage which determines the amount of foundation movement which can occur
d) soil permeability, affecting the moisture movements
e) climate, affecting the water input as rainfall and water loss in evaporation and transpiration
f) the water requirements of the tree
g) behaviour of the soil under load
h) behaviour of the building if stressed.

These factors will be considered in greater detail.

Rooting pattern of the tree
There is a popular misconception that some species of tree are 'tap-rooted' while others are shallow rooted. Regrettably, there is no such simplification. Another belief is that there is a relationship between tree height and root spread. This concept is fostered by the many recommendations and codes of practice which attempt to separate trees and buildings by a distance related to the tree height. An example is the National House Building Council Practice Note 3 which advocates an increase in depth of strip foundations if a tree is closer than its mature

height on a shrinkable clay soil, and even greater caution if the trees are in rows or groups.

This belief is perhaps a natural result from observing the aerial parts of a tree. An open-grown tree normally shows a neat symmetry, with a fixed ratio between height, branch spread and trunk diameter. The trunk and individual branches taper at a definable rate, and the whole system is anchored to the ground by the main roots forming a symmetical root plate. This rationalisation of the shape is a direct result of the forces acting on the trunk and branches. The most important of these are gravity and the stresses from wind, and the tree reacts to these in pre-determinable engineering terms.

By contrast, the feeder parts of the root system are supported by the soil and not subjected to external stresses. The factors controlling their development are the requirement of the roots for air (most roots require oxygen for aerobic respiration) and water, and the inability to penetrate very compacted soil. The root system will develop in response to the water demands of the aerial parts, with the roots extending along water gradients. Increasing distance from the trunk will increase the frictional resistance of water through the cellular vessels of the root, so placing limitations on the extent of lateral spread.

At the beginning of the summer, water will be absorbed from the surface zones of soil near the tree. As water deficits develop in this area, the zone of uptake progressively moves downwards and outwards, exploiting the most freely available water. If there is a ready supply of water (from rain or inflow from surrounding areas), the extent of root growth may be slight but, where extensive deficits develop, much greater root development will occur.

As the roots are exploiting areas of freely available water and oxygen, there is frequently a tendency for them to grow on the interface between a clay soil of low permeability and the topsoil or similar materials which permit rapid movements of air and water. Such conditions exist adjacent to foundations and in backfill soils from the laying of service trenches and so it is not surprising that extensive root activity occurs in such areas. Frequently, root samples are taken from these positions, and concern is expressed that these will damage the foundations or services. However, the roots may merely be exploiting these localised advantageous growing conditions and they are not necessarily either causing damage by shrinkage of the far deeper layers of soil beneath the foundations or damage to drains etc.

Bands of sand or similar materials of high permeability also provide a source of water in clay soils of otherwise low permeability. If the band of sand is of appreciable lateral extent, it can supply water from surrounding areas (assuming the correct conditions of drainage). Extra fine rooting will develop in this zone, and there will be a reduction in extent of other areas of rooting. Bands of sand of this type can be a frequent and important feature in minimizing the risks associated with glacial boulder clays and Oxford clay, but they probably also occur with other strata. They may have formed in glacial times as a result of the formation of extensive ice lenses within the permafrost soil, and these have subsequently filled with sand.

It must also be appreciated that the absorption of water occurs mainly in the hair roots which exploit the fine interstices between the soil particles. These only live for a short time (at most, one season) and are without cellular secondary thickening. They connect to slightly larger roots with secondary thickening, and these to progressively larger roots. Root samples taken for identification may be far removed from the area of active moisture uptake. Furthermore, the presence of a large root is not necessarily indicative that it is functional, as the water requirements of the tree may well be supplied by other, more readily available, sources of water.

This description of the root system emphasises that, although it develops in a strictly logical fashion, the outcome can be a most irregular system. The species of tree and parameters of crown size may dictate the water demand but they do not control the shape or extent of the root system.

Patterns of water deficit
The roots of a tree are only capable of causing subsidence of the foundation of a building by causing a soil to dry and shrink. As the development of the root system is so irregular and the mere presence of identifiable roots is no proof of their activity, it becomes more logical to measure their effects on the soil. The simplest method of achieving this is by taking soil samples, weighing them before and after oven drying (at 105°C to constant weight), and calculating the moisture content. If a soil is reasonably homogeneous, it becomes possible to compare the moisture content/depth profile between soils subject to root activity and adjacent areas beyond the spread of the roots. Examples of this are shown in figure **2.2.**

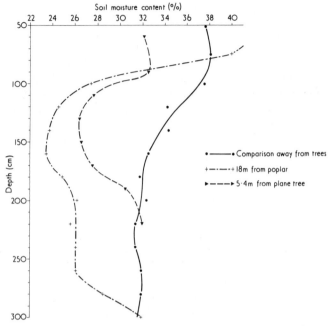

Fig. 2.2. Soil moisture profiles in proximity to different tree species on London clay (from Biddle[1])

This technique will only reveal the full extent of water deficit at a single time but, with experience and by examination of the extent of fine hair roots in the soil, it becomes possible to estimate the likely maximum deficits at other times of year.

A more sophisticated technique has been made possible by the development of the neutron probe. This requires the insertion of an aluminium access tube in a bore-hole carefully drilled in the soil, down which the probe is lowered. The probe contains a small radio-active source, emitting fast neutrons. If these collide with hydrogen atoms, they are slowed down and reflected, and the probe contains a counter for these slow-returning neutrons. As virtually the sole source of hydrogen atoms in the soil is in the form of water, the count of returning neutrons is proportional to the soil moisture-content. Measurements can be made at close intervals down the tube, permitting easy and precise definition of the moisture-content profile. The technique is particularly valuable for measuring the seasonal pattern of soil moisture changes in the vicinity of a tree, as repeated measurements can be made in the same hole. Figure **2.3** illustrates a typical result.

28

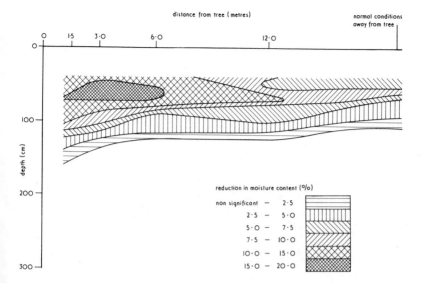

Fig. 2.3. Seasonal changes in water deficit, measured by neutron probe, 6m from a 10m high horse-chestnut on Oxford clay. (112cps approximately equal to 0.1 moisture volume fraction)

Although it has been emphasised that the root system, and thus water demand, is not necessarily regular and symmetrical around a tree, in homogeneous clay soils of low permeability a fairly regular system might be expected. If a degree of symmetry can be assumed, a series of access holes along a radius from a tree can indicate the patterns of water deficit surrounding the tree (figure **2.4**). By monitoring water deficits over several seasons, ideally including a period of fairly severe drought, it becomes possible to build up an accurate picture of the effects of the root system on soil moisture content.

Soil shrinkage
The dimensional changes which a clay soil undergoes when it is subject to changes in moisture content vary, depending on the clay.

Soil classification systems arbitrarily define clay particles as having an effective diameter of two microns (0.002 mm) or less, but particle size is only one of the variables in clay structure. Clays vary in their mineralogical composition, with differing

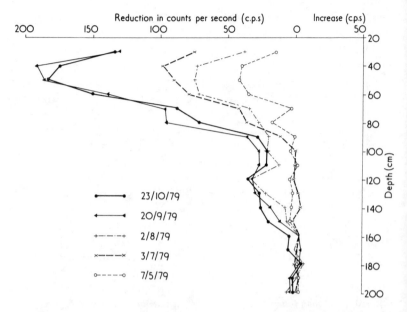

Fig. 2.4. Pattern of water deficit, measured by neutron probe, in the vicinity of a 15m high horse chestnut tree on boulder clay in September 1979

molecular lattice structures. Montmorillonite clay consists of a three-layer mineral, comprising a single layer of interlocking octahedra formed of an aluminium atom surrounded by six oxygen ions, sandwiched between two layers of interlocking tetrahedra formed of silica atoms surrounded by four oxygen ions. By contrast, kaolinite is a two-layer mineral, comprising a single layer of the aluminium octahedra and silica tetrahedra. These different structures have differing electro-static attraction for the sorbed water, and differing shrinkage properties.

Clays also have the ability to absorb and exchange cations, and the proportion of sorbed cations can affect their shrinkage. In particular, calcium ions decrease the soil volume changes. This property is utilised in clay stabilisation techniques.

Within the upper size limit of two microns, there are also variations in the size of the clay particles, down to colloidal material. The greater the colloidal fraction, the greater the potential for shrinkage movements. In practice, clay soils also contain a proportion of particles larger than 2 microns which are dimensionally stable. In particular, the sand-size grains from an

30

unshrinkable matrix, and the diameter and proportion of sand thus affects shrinkage.

Despite these enormous potential and practical differences in the behaviour of clay soils, there is a tendency to lump together all soils combining any proportion of clay as 'shrinkable clays'. Guide-lines and codes of practice do not attempt to make any distinction between differing clays, although the term 'heavy shrinkable clays' is sometimes used but without defining 'heavy'. These guide-lines have mostly been formulated on the basis of research work by W.H. Ward and are based on experience with the London clay. Their applicability to other clay soils is dubious. Recent work at the Royal Botanic Garden, Kew (Cutler and Richardson) has shown that 75 per cent of their enquiries for root identification come from London clay, with the remaining 25 per cent originating from a wide variety of both clay and other soils.

If the risks associated with trees are to be properly appreciated, it is essential to differentiate between the highly shrinkable clays, with associated high risks, and the less shrinkable clays with corresponding less risk.

There are many different methods of classifying potential shrinkability but, probably, the most widely accepted is by plasticity index. This has the advantage of being an easily and commonly measured parameter, and of reflecting many of the differences in clay composition. Other methods measure shrinkage limit, liquid limit, penetration resistance or swelling pressure. Holtz has proposed the following criteria for expansive soils. These would be equally applicable to shrinkage problems.

On the basis of these criteria, I would suggest that the major

TABLE 2.1   Criteria for defining shrinkability of clay soils

Degree of expansion or shrinkage	Plasticity index	Colloid content % (<0.001 mm)	Shrinkage limit
Very high	>35	>28	<11
High	25-41	20-31	7-12
Medium	15-28	13-23	10-16
Low	<18	<15	>15

problems of subsidence damage are associated with soils in the 'very high' category (plasticity index greater than 35). This would include the London clay (plasticity index normally between 40 and 60), which is the soil where problems occur most commonly. With soils of lower plasticity, there is a correspondingly lower risk, suggesting that the guide-lines relating tree height to distance from building should be relaxed.

Soil permeability

The rates of water movement through clay soils are very variable but, in general, the more shrinkable the soil, the lower the permeability. The soil structure, in particular the vertical and horizontal cracks, also has an enormous influence. Permeability affects the rate of lateral moisture migration towards zones of soil desiccation produced by root activity. Such movements may be very significant in sandy soils, but are of negligible significance in the more shrinkable clay soils. In these soils, gradients of water movement probably do not extend more than 30 cm beyond the zone of active water uptake by the roots. As a result, in impermeable clays, the trees will produce a bowl-shaped zone of soil desiccation around the trunk.

Permeability to vertical movements of water is also very important. The more permeable clays (e.g. boulder clay) allow the rainfall during winter months to penetrate the soil and correct any water deficits which might have been produced by root activity during the summer. In this situation, soil movements will show a simple seasonal cycle of swelling and shrinking, with a low amplitude of movement, as the soil is of low shrinkability. By contrast, with the less permeable clays, the winter rainfall will not penetrate to correct the deficits of the previous year. The next summer, any rain which has penetrated will be absorbed first, and root activity and soil desiccation will then have to extend further and deeper. As a result, the soil movements will consist of a seasonal pattern of swelling and shrinking (of high amplitude, if the low permeability is associated with high shrinkage), superimposed on a trend of progressively increasing shrinkage as the zone of desiccation extends.

This permanent water deficit will only be corrected when the tree dies, or water demand is significantly reduced. It is in these conditions that the serious problems of heave damage to foundations can occur. If a building is placed on the desiccated soil, as the soil rehydrates it will swell and lift the foundations, often causing serious structural damage. This can be avoided by leaving time for the soil to recover its normal moisture content but, with the impermeable clays, this takes many years. This is exemplified by the classic study on the cottages at Windsor, which continued to heave for more than 20 years after the felling of some mature elm trees (Samuels and Cheney).

Climate

Climate affects both the input and output in the soil water balance. The most important input of water for the soil is from rainfall, and output as evapotranspiration is influenced by the amount of sunshine, radiation, air temperature and windspeed. The Meteorological Office regularly monitors these parameters in their weather-recording stations, and these data can be used in calculations of the potential evapotranspiration and soil-moisture deficits.

Soil-moisture deficits are considered to have been set up when evapotranspiration exceeds rainfall, and vegetation has to draw on reserves of water in the soil to satisfy transpiration requirements. The assessment of soil-moisture deficit takes account of the fact that vegetation has increasing difficulty in extracting moisture from the soil. For this, it is assumed that short-rooted vegetation (grass etc) can draw up to 75mm of water from the soil before actual evapotranspiration starts falling below its potential, and that long-rooted vegetation (trees etc) can draw on 200mm of soil moisture. In the calculations of moisture deficit, allowance is made for the extent to which actual evapotranspiration falls below its potential when the difference (evaporation minus rainfall) exceeds 75mm in areas of short-rooted vegetation, or 200mm with long-rooted vegetation.

The calculations of moisture deficit provide a measure of the extent to which the soil can dry out as a result of evaporation of water and the transpirational effects of grass and trees. This is probably the most relevant method of defining the dryness or droughtiness of the weather.

Using this concept, figure **2.5** shows the frequency with which precipitation deficits exceed 200mm in Great Britain. In these areas, if tree root activity is present, soil moisture deficits over 200mm could be anticipated. It illustrates that, over most of the country, deficits greater than 200mm occur less than once in ten years but that, around the Thames Estuary, deficits of this magnitude occur between 7 and 9 times in 10 years. It shows that the

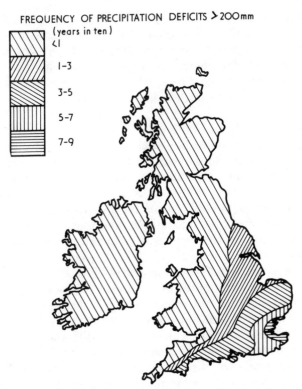

FREQUENCY OF PRECIPITATION DEFICITS > 200mm
(years in ten)

< 1

1–3

3–5

5–7

7–9

Fig. 2.5. Geographical distribution of the frequency of maximum precipitation deficits of 200mm or more (from Mohrmann and Kessler)

area at greatest risk is the south-east of England.

The parameter which accounts for the greatest variation in soil-moisture deficit is the rainfall. This can vary from +70 per cent to −40 per cent of the mean annual value (Glasspole). By comparison, potential evaporation only varies by a factor of 20 per cent of the mean. Not surprisingly, therefore, it is periods of low rainfall which have the greatest influence in determining the amount of deficit.

These theoretical considerations of water deficit are of only limited value in any detailed analysis of the drying pattern around individual trees. The use of a constant of 200mm for the maximum water deficit produced by tree roots fails to take account of any variation between species in the volume of soil which it exploits, or of the size of the tree. Furthermore, as it is the conditions of extreme drought which give rise to the greatest

34

risk of structural damage, it is relevant to determine the precise extent to which trees of differing size and species exploit the soil, and their efficiency at increasing their rooting zone under such conditions. Data on these aspects is not available, and can only come from more detailed research such as measurement of water deficits around trees using the neutron probe.

Water requirements of the tree

It is essential to appreciate that about 99.9 per cent of water demand of a tree is required to meet the transpirational losses and it is, therefore, necessary to understand this fundamental plant function.

The materials required for plant growth are synthesised in the chloroplasts of the leaf, using the energy of sunlight to convert carbon dioxide and water to sugar (the process of photosynthesis). Carbon dioxide is absorbed in the film of moisture which covers the mesophyll cells of the inner leaf. It enters the leaf through minute pores – the stomata – but it is equally possible for the moisture to evaporate from the mesophyll cells and diffuse out through the stomata. This process is known as transpiration. The opening and closing of the stomata is controlled by a pair of guard cells, the function of which is dependent upon the turgidity of the leaf. If transpiration is too rapid for the supply, turgidity is lost and the stomata close, thereby preventing further water loss and stopping carbon dioxide assimilation and photosynthesis. It can be appreciated from this that there is a relationship between growth and transpiration loss, and evidence exists of variation between species in their efficiency at producing sugars per unit loss of water.

This efficiency is only one of the many factors involved. Obviously, leaf area is of fundamental importance, as this controls the potential transpiring surface. Temperature, sunshine, wind and atmospheric vapour pressure influence the rate of transpiration, and the shape, density and exposure of the tree crown determine the manner in which the leaf area is presented to these climatic factors.

The effects of this variation in the water demand of different tree species has previously been illustrated in figure **2.2**, which shows the water deficits in the vicinity of a poplar and of a plane tree. It shows the enormously greater water demand of poplar, a fact which is reflected in the various codes of practice concerning proximity of trees to buildings, which normally consider poplar, willow and elm to pose particular problems. There is very little detailed comparative data of the water requirements of other species, but various lists exist which attempt to place trees in a rank order, based on the personal experience of the observers. Table 2.2 shows three such lists, and demonstrates that there are many similarities between these lists. However, there are also important differences, but these may be reflecting different experiences of the observers as much as inherent differences of species or site. Data of this type based on observations on non-comparable sites and conditions can never produce satisfactory guide-lines, and a proper experimental approach is required.

Behaviour of soil under load

The load of a building on any soil will give rise to some settlement movements, but these are particularly important on cohesive clay soils. Foundation design aims to ensure that the movements are within the limits that can be tolerated by the structure without adversely affecting its functional requirements.

Foundation design on clay soils should calculate the ultimate bearing capacity of the soil, and incorporate an adequate factor of safety. Failure to do so can result in shear failure of the soil, but problems of this type are unusual. However, foundations on cohesive soils are also subject to settlement movements related to volume changes. These consist of the immediate or elastic settlement which occurs immediately upon load application, and the primary consolidation settlement which develops when the volume changes as a consequence of draining of water from the soil voids under the influence of the applied load. With soils of low permeability, this consolidation settlement can take many years to complete and, with some soils, secondary consolidation settlement can continue almost indefinitely.

Although correct foundation design should ensure that all these load-induced movements occur evenly so as to produce uniform settlement, inevitably, they will tend to produce some stressing of the fabric and, in some cases, severe fracturing. This must be distinguished from problems associated with soil shrinkage resulting from changes in soil moisture content produced by root activity.

These different types of movement can frequently be distinguished by monitoring the seasonal pattern of levels or crack movements. Damage caused by consolidation settlement will be irreversible, and the cracks will progressively increase in width, particularly during winter months. By contrast, clay shrinkage will normally show a distinct pattern of seasonal movement, with cracks opening during the summer when the clay shrinks, and

Table 2.2 **Comparison of lists by different authors showing rank order of water demand of different species of tree**

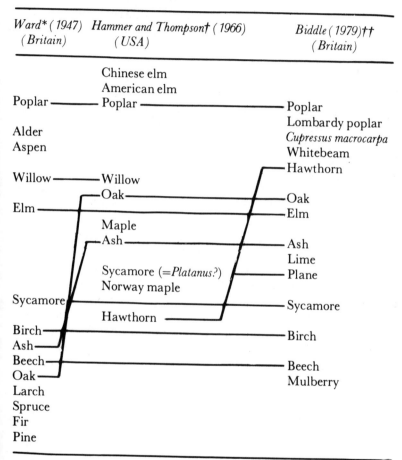

Ward* (1947) (Britain)	Hammer and Thompson† (1966) (USA)	Biddle (1979)†† (Britain)
	Chinese elm	
	American elm	
Poplar ———	Poplar ———————————	Poplar
Alder		Lombardy poplar
Aspen		*Cupressus macrocarpa*
		Whitebeam
		Hawthorn
Willow ———	Willow	
	Oak	Oak
Elm		Elm
	Maple	
	Ash	Ash
		Lime
	Sycamore (=*Platanus?*)	Plane
	Norway maple	
Sycamore		Sycamore
	Hawthorn ———	
Birch		Birch
Ash		
Beech		Beech
Oak		Mulberry
Larch		
Spruce		
Fir		
Pine		

* Ward, W.H. The effects of fast growing trees and shrubs on shallow foundations. *Journ. Inst. Landsc. Archit.*, 1947, 11, 4, 7-16
† Hammer, M.J., and Thompson, O.B. Foundation clay shrinkage caused by large trees. *Journ. Soil. Mech.*, Foundns. Div., Proc. Amer. Soc. Civ. Engrs., 1966, *92*, 11-17.
†† See note 1 on p. 47.

closing during the winter when the clay rehydrates and swells. With stiff and over-consolidated clays, these swelling pressures generate enormous pressures and can be sufficient to lift the building back to its original level.

In practice, foundation movements on clay soils in the vicinity of trees tend to be a combination of both shrinkage and consolidation settlement. When the soil dries and shrinks, the building will subside. When it rehydrates, the soil must not only support the weight of the building but must also transmit the increased pressures generated by the swelling of the soil. These increased pressures will increase the consolidation, and with soft soils can also result in the ultimate soil bearing capacity being exceeded, so that shear failure occurs. In these situations, the recovery movements will be less than the soil shrinkage and, over a period of years, this can gradually accumulate until damage finally develops.

Cumulative movements of this type are particularly serious on soft clay or silt soils. Even if the clay is of inherently low shrinkage characteristics, they can gradually give rise to massive amounts of movement and damage, particularly where the foundations are to minimum specification.

Behaviour of building when stressed

Although the soil may shrink when subjected to drying, or consolidate under load, the development of damage ultimately depends on the reaction of the building to such soil movements. If these movements are uniform over the whole building, no stresses are set up and no damage occurs. It is only when there is differential movement that damage occurs. Differential movements are normally measured as angular distortions. Modern brickwork and plaster quickly show the effects of differential movements, and the onset of cracking can be expected with an angular distortion of 1/300. This is equivalent to a differential movement of 10mm over a span of 3m. By comparison, in Victorian buildings, lime mortar and sand were normally used for the bonding of the bricks, and this is far more flexible.

The risks of damage are closely related to the shape and construction of the building. Buildings with a rectangular box section are far less liable to damage than irregularly-shaped buildings, in which differential movements can easily occur between the different sections. Localised projections on a building are frequently damaged if they are more subject than the main building

38

to movements from soil shrinkage. Examples of this are bay windows, which may be projecting on the house frontage, and are particularly prone to damage caused by trees in the adjacent street. Damage of this sort is the most commonly occurring type on pre-war buildings in terrace and semi-detached housing.

Buildings with extensions are particularly vulnerable. The extensions are normally added when the foundation settlement movements of the main building have finished, but the extension is still subject to its initial settlement. This causes initial stressing at the junction between the extension and original building, and any further slight movements, such as seasonal shrinkage and swelling caused by trees, can be sufficient to trigger off damage. Damage of this type can be avoided by including slip joints at the junctions of extensions.

THE PREVENTION OR AVOIDANCE OF TREE ROOT DAMAGE

The conflict between trees and building can arise in different ways, and these require different solutions to overcome the problems.

The conflict can arise with a new building and new planting, a new building and existing trees, an existing building and new trees, or an existing building and existing trees.

The solution to all of these problems in the past has tended to be attempts to separate trees and building. Such recommendations are embodied in the National House Building Council Practice Note 3, Building Research Digest No. 63 (Soils and Foundations: 1), and in British Standards Institution Code of Practice for Foundations (BS CP 2004: 1972). All of these guides refer to problems occurring with either heavy or firm shrinkable clays, but make no attempt to define the term 'heavy' or the amount of shrinkage. As a result, there is a tendency for any soil with cohesive properties to be described as clay and, in many cases, even non-shrinkable sandy soils are mis-identified as clay. This frequently gives rise to wholly unjustifiable concern about the proximity of trees to buildings.

These ambiguities can be avoided by defining the extent of the problem, in particular the shrinkability of the clay, and the extent of water deficit of the tree on this particular clay type. Although current knowledge may be insufficient to distinguish between the extent of water deficit of different tree species, there are no such problems with clay shrinkage. Table 2.1 gives a basis for classification of shrinkability, and practical experience suggests that the serious problems only occur with the clays of the 'very shrinkable' category, which have a plasticity index over 35.

Possible methods of preventing or avoiding the risks of damage, in situations where genuine problem conditions exist, are considered below.

New buildings and new planting

The maximum number of options is available for avoiding damage where it is possible to control both the trees and the buildings.

Increasing the depth of foundations so as to take them below the depth of soil shrinkage is undoubtedly the most effective solution, and is advocated by the National House Building Council Practice Note 3, which provides for increasing depth of traditional strip foundations. The Building Research Digest 67 (Soils and Foundations: 3) recommends the use of bored piles and ground beams, and this would appear to be the most effective solution. Regrettably, it has not been widely adopted, mainly because of reluctance to incur the slightly greater initial costs of such foundations, without appreciating the additional safety which is obtained with this system.

Despite the widespread appreciation of the advantages of improved foundations, builders and architects tend to be very short-sighted and provide for foundations of the minimum specifications, which is only applicable for conditions occurring at the time of construction. No allowance is made for planting trees at some time in the future, or for the possibility of self-sown trees becoming established during the life of the building. If builders are going to be so short-sighted, it behoves our planners to adopt a more responsible attitude. Section 59 of the Town and Country Planning Act 1971 imposes such requirements by stating 'It shall be the duty of the local planning authority to ensure, whenever it is appropriate, that in granting planning permission for any development adequate provision is made, by the imposition of conditions for the preservation or planting of trees'. If such planting requires improved foundations, conditions to that effect should be enforced, and Section D3 of the Building Regulations requires this by stipulating that: 'The foundations of a building shall be taken down to such a depth, or

40

be so constructed, as to safeguard the building against damage by swelling or shrinking or the subsoil'. Thus, the means are available for enforcing stringent conditions for foundation design to ensure that tree-planting can occur without risk at any time in the future.

If, despite the importance of building with adequate foundations, this precaution is omitted, the risks of damage can be reduced by selecting species with an inherently low water demand. Table 2.2 provides an indication of those species with apparently lower requirements, which should be preferred in the vicinity of buildings, while poplars, with their exceptionally high water demand, should be kept well away. Unfortunately, the existing lists are inadequate, both in the number of tree species included and in the amount of information concerning the patterns of water demand of these trees. It is to be hoped that research will provide more accurate guide-lines in the future, and may even permit the selection of varieties with lower water requirement.

New buildings with existing trees

Where trees are already present on a building site, slightly different precautions are required. The risks of soil shrinkage due to the future water demand of the trees can be overcome by increased foundation depths, and similar criteria for this would apply to those for new buildings and new plantings.

However, there can be other problems if the existing trees have already caused some drying of the subsoil. If the foundations are placed on this soil, when the trees are removed, either to permit the development or because of their death at some time in the future, this desiccated soil will rehydrate. This will be accompanied by swelling of the soil, generating very considerable swelling pressures. If these are greater than the foundation loading, the foundations will 'heave' and this can give rise to serious damage. The extent of heave damage will be related to the zone of soil in which the swelling pressures exceed the foundation load and, with over-consolidated clays such as London clay, this can be almost as great an area as that affected by shrinkage. Problems of heave are not necessarily restricted to the immediate vicinity of the stump.

Heave damage can sometimes be avoided by felling trees and leaving sufficient time for the soil to rehydrate and swell before building commences. However, with soils of low permeability,

41

such as is the case usually with the shrinkable clays, the process of rehydration can take many years and cause unacceptable delays before building can start. The alternative is to design the foundations to accommodate the heave. This usually entails reinforced bored-piles of sufficient length, with the top 3m sleeved to permit movement of the surface soil, and with suspended ground beams and floors. Unless beams and floors are suspended, there is a risk that the building will be lifted off the piles.

New planting near existing buildings
If the existing buildings are on shallow foundations, the only way of achieving suitable planting in the close vicinity of the building is by the selection of trees of low water demand. The problems of this approach have already been mentioned.

Existing trees near existing buildings
The risks of existing trees near buildings are often first appreciated when structural damage develops. Once this has happened, various solutions are appropriate. Firstly, if the damage is not serious, it may be possible to curtail the future water demand and prevent exacerbation of the damage. In this respect, it should be noted that most of the damage caused by soil shrinkage by tree roots is of a comparatively minor nature. Table 2.3 presents the suggestions of the Buildings Research Establishment (Tomlinson et al), on the significance of cracks, and emphasises that most damage is only cosmetic and does not require extensive repairs. It is most exceptional for buildings to reach the stage of cracks wider than 25mm, where structural integrity is affected.

Water demand can be curtailed either by control of the leaf area or by limiting the root spread. As virtually all water loss occurs through the leaves as transpiration, control of the leaf area provides an obvious means of restricting water loss. This can be achieved by regular pruning.

The value of this technique can be appreciated by considering figure **2.6**. This shows a histogram of the annual growth increment (breast-height, basal area increment) of a typical plane tree in a London street, and is based on measurements of the width of annual rings in a sample taken with a Pressler increment borer. The tree was planted circa 1905 and, for the first few years, the rate of growth increased but, from 1910 to 1945,

Table 2.3 Classification of visible damage to walls with particular reference to ease of repair of plaster and brickwork, or masonry

Category of damage	Degree of Damage	Description of typical damage* (ease of repair in italics)	Approximate crack width (mm)†
0		Hairline cracks less than about 0.1 mm wide are classed as negligible	⊉ 0.1
1	Very slight	*Fine cracks which can easily be treated during normal decoration.* Perhaps isolated slight fracturing in building. Cracks rarely visible in external brickwork.	⊉ 1.0
2	Slight	*Cracks easily filled. Redecoration probably required. Recurrent cracks can be masked by suitable linings.* Cracks not necessarily visible externally: *some external repointing may be required to ensure weathertightness.* Doors and windows may stick slightly.	⊉ 5.0
3	Moderate	*The cracks require some opening up and can be patched by a mason. Repointing of external brickwork and possibly a small amount of brickwork to be replaced.* Doors and windows sticking. Service pipes may fracture. Weathertightness often impaired.	5 to 15 (or a number of cracks ⩾ 3.0)
4	Severe	*Extensive repair work involving breaking-out and replacing sections of walls, especially over doors and windows.* Window and door frames distorted, floor sloping noticeably.†† Walls leaning†† or bulging noticeably, some loss of bearing in beams. Service pipes disrupted.	15 to 25 but also depends on number of cracks

Continued

43

Degree of damage		Description of typical damage* (ease of repair in italics)	Approximate crack width (mm)†
5	Very severe	*This requires a major repair job involving partial or complete re-building.* Beams lose bearings, walls lean badly and require shoring. Windows broken with distortion. Danger of instability.	usually > 25 but depends on number of cracks

* It must be emphasised that in assessing the degree of damage account must be taken of the location in the building or structure where it occurs, and also of the function of the building or structure.

† Crack width is one factor in assessing degree of damage and should not be used on its own as a direct measure of it.

†† Local deviations of slope, from the horizontal or vertical, of more than 1/100, will normally be clearly visible. Overall deviations of over 1/150 are undesirable.

This table is extracted from Tomlinson et al.

growth remained fairly uniform at between 1,000 and 2,000mm² per annum. This was a result of a policy of heavy annual pruning, usually involving the removal of all shoots (the dotted line shows the trend that might be anticipated in the absence of pruning). During the war years, the growth rapidly increased as a result of lack of pruning but again was brought under control in the 1950s and 1960s. The most dramatic change has occurred during the past decade, with growth rate increasing to 7,300mm² in 1977. This is a direct result of the recent change in arboricultural policy brought about by pressure from amenity societies, to allow trees to grow a larger and more natural crown shape, and from cut-backs in local-authority expenditure on tree pruning.

The relationship between growth rate and water demand has previously been emphasised. Figure **2.6** demonstrates that the water demand of these trees must have increased substantially in recent years, while their roots must have extended further and deeper in their search for water. These results suggest that these trees were liable to cause damage during virtually any dry

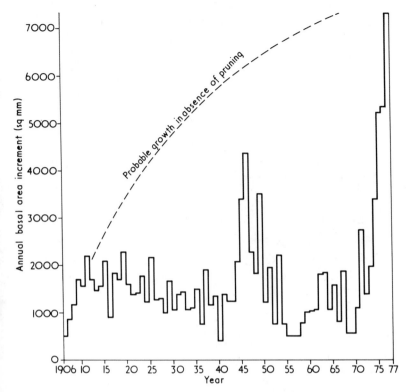

Fig. 2.6. Histogram showing annual growth rate of typical street-side plane tree in London

summer, without requiring the extreme conditions of 1976.

The obvious lesson to be learnt is to control the growth rate, and thus the water demand, by pruning and to vary the intensity of pruning to suit the vulnerability of the adjacent buildings. In figure **2.7** the effects are shown of heavy, medium and light pruning at the end of 1977. During 1978, the basal area increment was reduced to 1,100, 3,050 and 4,700mm^2, respectively. The appearance of these different pruning regimes is illustrated in Plates **21** and **23**.

The alternative is to limit root spread, but this has many problems. Physical root barriers, such as concrete or sheet piling, must extend beyond the range of root spread, both laterally and vertically. An inadequate barrier, which allows even a single root to penetrate to the distal side, will rapidly result in complete exploitation of the available moisture as if the

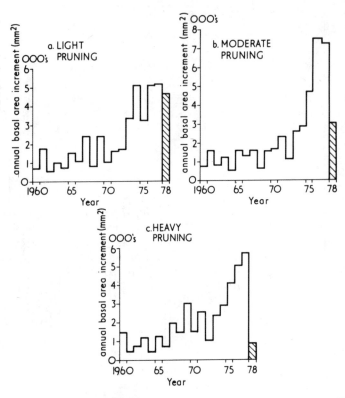

Fig. 2.7. Histograms to show the effect of varying pruning intensities in 1977 on the growth rate in 1978 (hatched)

barrier did not exist. It can thus provide a false sense of security at considerable cost. Possibly, a more effective method would be to kill the roots, using a chemical soil sterilant, such as metham sodium. This is the material used for control of root transmission of elm disease but it is still experimental for this situation. Holes are drilled at the appropriate depth and spacing (dependent on the proximity and species of tree, and the soil permeability). The soil sterilant is then added, to kill the roots which cross the barrier. The sterilant is biodegradable and, after several weeks, roots will again start to exploit the soil on the distal side. At suitable time intervals, any new roots can be killed, using the original boreholes, which should be filled with pea-grit. This technique has the advantage of encouraging the roots to develop through the barrier where they can be controlled, whereas the physical barrier must prevent any risk of being by-passed.

Provided the further soil movements can be prevented, either by removing the trees or curtailing their water demand, it should be possible to repair the damage without resorting to underpinning of the foundations. It is sometimes claimed that any cracking of the foundations has affected their strength but, unless the foundations are reinforced, they are not intended to confer rigidity to the building. Their function is purely to transmit the load of the building to the soil. Cracking of the brickwork will reduce its strength, but modern methods of resin bonding can produce a repair stronger than the original brickwork and, with careful stitching and repointing, can reinstate the building to its original condition.

However, there are many situations where further foundation movement cannot be prevented and where it is necessary to resort to underpinning of the foundations. Provided such repair carries all the foundations to sufficient depth to avoid any soil shrinkage below their base, it should be possible to retain trees, just as if the building had originally been constructed on adequate deep foundations. However, wherever partial underpinning is carried out, there may be a continuing risk of soil shrinkage beneath those areas not underpinned and it may still be necessary to fell the trees which could affect these areas.

REFERENCES

1 P.G. Biddle, Tree root damage to buildings: an arboriculturist's experience, *Arboric. Journ.*, 1979, **3**, 6, 397-412
2 D. Cutler and I.B.K. Richardson, *Trees and buildings,* Hornby, Lancs, Construction Press (in press)
3 J. Glasspole, The reliability of rainfall over the British Isles, *J. Instn. Wat. Engrs.*, 1951, **5**, 6, 17-38
4 W.G. Holtz, Expansive clay: properties and problems, *Colorado School of Mines Quarterly*, 1959, **54**, no 4
5 J.C.J. Mohrmann and J. Kessler, Water deficiences in European agriculture, *Int. Inst. Land Reclamation and Improvement*, 1959, Publ. no 5
6 S.G. Samuels and J.E. Cheney, Long-term heave of a building on clay due to tree removal, *Sym. British Geotech. Soc.*, 1974, 212-220
7 M.J. Tomlinson, R. Driscoll and J.B. Burland, *Foundations for low-rise buildings,* 1978, BRE Current Paper, CP 61/78
8 W.H. Ward, Soil movement and weather, *Proc. 3rd Int. Conf. Soil Mech. and Found. Eng.*, 1953, **1**, 477-482

3
The care and repair of trees

Peter Bridgeman

INTRODUCTION

Many of our towns and cities have inherited a wealth of fine trees. These trees can form the backbone of our town landscape and provide great amenity. There are, however, many physical and pathological problems with trees in towns and this chapter suggests how careful and skilful tree surgery can often reduce the problems which trees can create.

Many of these large trees were planted last century and are either now too large for the existing surroundings or are at, or past, maturity. The nineteenth-century planting was often carried out by enthusiastic but untrained staff and the main fault was the selection of large-growing forest-type trees for planting in confined areas close to buildings. The economic pressures of the first half of the twentieth century meant that little money or expertise was afforded to tree-planting and care and, by 1950, many of our towns inherited serious problems of a town treescape made up of large neglected trees and little replacement planting.

Since the 1950s, we have seen an increase in home ownership, more enlightened town planning by the authorities and a greater awareness of the importance of trees in our landscape by planners and architects. The individual home-owners, with more money and leisure time, have planted trees and shrubs in front gardens, giving a great variety of shapes and colours. In some cases, there have been too many Kanzan Cherries planted at the expense of other small trees but, generally, the town-house treescape has improved.

More and more local authorities have appointed professionally trained forestry and arboricultural staff, and this has resulted in improved standards of selection, planting and maintenance of trees in housing estates, parks and schools, and on highways.

The greater awareness of the importance of trees has resulted in increased legislation to encourage planting and protection of trees, and the public, through civic and amenity societies, have helped by acting as watchdogs where trees are threatened. Dutch elm disease, although a major landscape disaster in most of the southern half of Britain, has again reinforced the importance of trees and made everyone aware of how vulnerable and fragile is our treescape.

We still have too many landscapes where the majority of the trees are at, or past, maturity and with planting only of small trees. This age/size imbalance needs correcting over the next twenty-five years if we are to have an acceptable town treescape for the twenty-first century.

FORMULATION OF TOWN TREE POLICY

Every parish, ward, town or city should have an overall tree policy to plan future planting, maintenance and necessary feeling. Such a policy should be initiated and co-ordinated by the district or borough council, but the parish councils, local civic or amenity societies and other voluteer groups can help in the collecting of essential data.

Tree surveys
The first essential in the formulation of an overall tree policy is to know the positions, species, sizes and condition of the existing trees. Such information needs to be collected accurately and updated regularly. The compilation of a tree survey of a complete town may sound daunting but, if divided into areas, wards or even individual parks, streets etc, the footwork can be shared.

The master plan would be prepared by the professional staff of the local authority and help in the survey can be enlisted from local voluntary groups.

The amount of detail required must be determined at the outset but, if the survey is going to be of value, it must give sufficient information to plan a future management policy. The Tree Council produces a very useful leaflet *Tree surveys* available from The Tree Council, 35 Belgrave Square, London, SW1X 8QN.

49

Management policy

Once the existing treescape has been surveyed and recorded, it is necessary to plan for a future tree-management policy. This policy must take into account trees on local-authority land, highways, and trees in private ownership.

The survey will highlight planting, maintenance and felling requirements, these should be phased into the management plan. Trees on privately-owned land can be considered for protection by Tree Preservation Orders; dangerous trees can be felled.

By involving the local civic and amenity societies in the preparation of the survey, it will be possible to keep them better informed as to the objectives of a management plan and they should then appreciate the need for necessary felling and replanting.

Once a policy has been formulated, it can be related to the necessary financial provision for direct labour, contractors, supply of trees and equipment.

TREE INSPECTIONS

Trees growing in towns are liable to damage from a vast range of natural and man-made agencies and, at any time during their lifespan, they may require treatment and, ultimately, felling.

Every tree owner has the legal obligation to inspect regularly his trees to ensure the safety of surrounding features and the public. If a tree, or part of a tree, does fall and injure a person or damage property, the questions will be asked 'Was the tree showing symptoms of weakness before the accident?' and 'Had the tree been inspected?'. The damaged party will have to prove the tree owner negligent and this would not be difficult if the tree was dead, or there were large dead branches in the crown, major cavities or severe root damage.

Some trees could develop serious structural weaknesses without obvious external symptoms and, in the event of an accident, the courts would have to decide whether the weakness could and should have been recognised by inspection.

Many local authorities have their own professionally-trained arboricultural staff for work planning and control, and tree inspections. There are still, however, many county and district councils which do not have such expertise on hand.

The private tree-owner has the same responsibility to inspect and maintain his trees and, although he could recognise the very

50

obvious faults, he may well have to call in a consultant to advise in detail.

The frequency of the inspections will depend on the size and position of the tree but large mature trees close to buildings or roads should be checked twice a year; once in summer when the leaves can be inspected and dead wood easily recognised, and again in winter to check the overall shape and condition of the branches. The inspector will need to be familiar with the normal characteristics of the trees and be able to spot abnormalities and weaknesses.

All parts of the tree should be examined, including leaves, branch structure, trunk and roots. If internal rots are suspected, these can be confirmed by drilling into the trunk with an auger.

The Forestry Commission/D.O.E. produce a useful leaflet – *The external signs of decay in trees : Arboricultural Leaflet No. 1.1977.*

For those in need of professional advice for tree inspection, the Arboricultural Association issues free the publication, *Directory of Consultants and Contractors for Tree Work.*

TREE PRUNING AND REPAIR

Trees growing in natural conditions can, and have, survived without the help of man for many millions of years. However, where trees are standing amongst buildings and roads, and in small gardens, they are often affected by man's activities and, therefore, require man's help.

Trees which have outgrown their situation, trees damaged by storm, vandals, faulty workmanship or pests and diseases can often be pruned or repaired by skilful tree surgery.

The recognition of damage and faults requires a great deal of expertise, and the justification for tree surgery must be balanced against costs and the value of the tree. Much of the work is also potentially very dangerous for the operators, public and surrounding property.

This chapter outlines the main operations of tree pruning, remedial and preventative tree surgery and tree felling. It concludes with a summary of the safety aspects involved and the employment of staff for this skilful work.

TREE PRUNING

Careful and judicious pruning can improve the appearance of trees, lessen the nuisance caused by shade and leaves, make the

51

trees safer and prolong their useful life. Unskilled work can completely ruin in minutes what has taken years to grow. Tree pruning is irreversible and dangerous, so only competent, experienced staff should carry out the work. The following pruning operations should be considered:

Formative pruning

When trees are purchased from nurseries and planted in towns, it is important to check that the shape and balance of the trunk and branches are correct to ensure acceptable growth. With large-growing trees, it is important to form a good sturdy trunk, a well-balanced and even branch-spread and one clear central leader. A few minutes with a pair of secateurs could save hours or even days of work later in the tree's life.

All broken and crossing branches or twigs should be removed, cutting back to the trunk or stem. If there is more than one leader the best should be selected and the others pruned out (see figure **3.1**). If feathered trees are planted (branches to ground

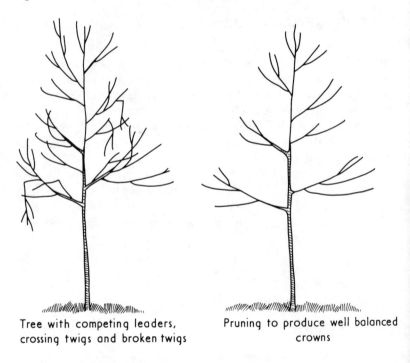

Tree with competing leaders,
crossing twigs and broken twigs

Pruning to produce well balanced
crowns

Fig. 3.1.   Formative pruning

52

level), it must be decided if this low cover is required for screening purposes or if access is required under the tree. If low lateral branches are to be removed, it may be necessary to cut them back to two or three buds in the first year to allow the trunk to expand (see figure **3.2**). All cuts should be made flush to the trunk or stem, or to a growing bud, and painted.

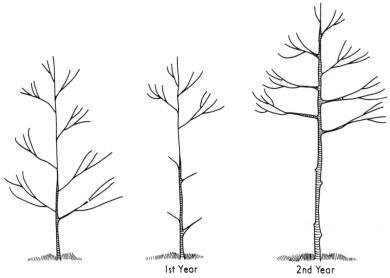

1st Year   2nd Year

Fig. 3.2. Pruning 'feathered' tree to 'standard' over two seasons. 1st year: lower laterals cut back to 2 or 3 buds to help thicken stem. 2nd year: lateral spurs removed and crown developing

As trees establish and grow, checks should be made to maintain well-balanced branch systems.

Cleaning out or removing dead wood
As trees mature, they often have dead branches, or rubbish or climbing plants can develop in the crown. Removing dead wood and unwanted rubbish or plants will help reduce the likelihood of disease becoming established and, obviously, makes the tree safer.

All dead wood should be removed back to sound wood and cut flush to the trunk or branch.

Crown thinning
In conjunction with cleaning out, it is often necessary to thin out

53

the branches in the crown of the tree. This may involve the removal of a percentage of live, healthy branches. If carried out carefully, it will leave the tree's natural size and shape but reduce the density of the tree, thereby allowing more light and wind through it.

If trees have been weakened by root damage or rots in the trunk, branch thinning will also reduce the wind catchment area, thus making the tree safer.

The thinning should be carried out throughout the branch system by first removing any weak or crossing branches and then removing a percentage of the live wood to achieve the desired degree of thinning.

Crown lifting
Trees with lower branches can obstruct vehicular and pedestrian access and buildings, and block views. Careful removal of lower branches can reduce these problems but still leave a natural-looking tree. Sometimes, entire branches can be removed back to the trunk or, alternatively, low branches can be pruned back to the branch above (see figure **3.3**).

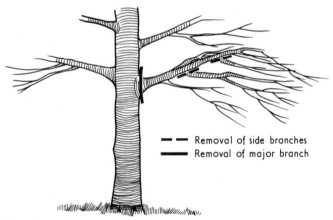

Removal of side branches
Removal of major branch

Fig. 3.3. Crown lifting, to give access or view under tree

Some trees, particularly many conifers, look better with branches to ground level and their shape may be spoiled by severe lifting.

Reducing and shaping
Where trees have completely outgrown their situation and are

54

causing serious problems by their size, it is sometimes possible to reduce the overall height and/or spread by skilful crown-reduction. Many broad-crowned trees can be reduced by shortening the branches back to other growing branches. This work needs careful control from ground level to ensure the tree's overall shape is maintained (see figure **3.4**). Sometimes,it is necessary to cut back further and leave stumps. This will look unsightly for a few years but vigorous healthy trees will soon produce growth from the cut stumps.

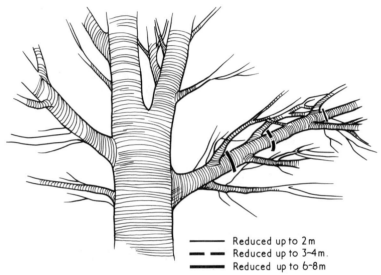

Reduced up to 2 m
Reduced up to 3–4 m.
Reduced up to 6–8 m

Fig. 3.4. Crown reduction: example of one branch reduced by cutting back to growing branches or main stems

Severe lopping should be avoided wherever possible but, if it is the only method because of surrounding features or rots in the upper crown, it may be better than complete removal.

Crown renewal
When trees have been severely lopped or pollarded, it is some-times possible to re-form an acceptable new crown from the resulting re-growth. This operation, is quite common with street trees, where trees such as limes and planes have been pollarded year after year. Checks should be made to ensure that the old stumps are not rotten and, if sound, one, two or three shoots per

stump can be retained to form a new crown. Further thinning of these shoots may be required after a year or two of growth (see Plate **25.**).

Branch removal

Any branch to be removed should, where possible, be cut flush to the branch or trunk from which it was growing and treated with an approved tree paint.

If there is clear ground beneath the tree, the branch can be severed and allowed to drop but, if there are fittings, features or other branches underneath it may be necessary to secure the branches with ropes and lower them carefully to the ground.

Basic branch removal should be carried out by a three-cut technique.

The first cut is made on the underside of the branch,cutting about one-quarter to one-third of the branch diameter. This will prevent the branch from tearing when the top severing-cut is made. This first cut is positioned about 1ft to 2ft away from the main trunk or branch (see figure **3.5**). The second cut is positioned a further $\frac{1}{2}$in to 2in further out along the branch and is cut from the top, parallel to the first undercut (see figure **3.6**). The branch will break cleanly along the grain when the second cut is parallel to the first cut.

The third 'flush' cut is made from the top and severs the stump flush to the trunk. The final cut surface should be as small as possible but not leaving a stump (see figure **3.7**).

With the use of a lightweight chain-saw,it is easy to over-flush the final cut and this results in a very large wound which will take many years to heal and, therefore, will be more liable to infection from wood-rotting fungi.

Lowering branches

Lowering branches with ropes is a more involved process and usually means passing a heavy rope through a high fork in the crown and attaching one end to the branch to be removed, the other end being used to lower the severed branch carefully to the ground. On occasions, two ropes are required or, alternatively, the branch is taken off in several small sections.

Tree paints

All final cuts over 2in diameter on large trees, and $\frac{1}{2}$in diameter when carrying out formative pruning on young trees, should be

Plate 1. *What would Durham be like without its tree-cloaked outcrop to enhance the cathedral? Photo: Aerofilms Ltd*

Plate 2. *Trees form an attractive winter landscape in Lynn Park, Glasgow. Photo: The Architectural Press. Photographer: Sam Lambert*

Plate 3, 4. St. Paul's churchyard, Covent Garden. Imagine it without the trees.
Photo: The Tree Council. Photographer: David Trace

Plate 5. Jardin des Plantes, Paris. A magnificent avenue of pruned trees. Photo: The Architectural Press. Photographer: Sherban Cantacuzino.

Plate 6. Hyde Park, London. A green wedge within the dense urban development.
Photo: Aerofilms Ltd

Plate 7. Kensington, London: green tree-filled squares break up the built areas.
Photo: Aerofilms Ltd

Plate 8. Welwyn Garden City. Tree-lined avenues, gardens, and woodlands.
Photo: Aerofilms Ltd

Plate 9. Letchworth Garden City. Photo: Aerofilms Ltd

Plate 10. Harlow New Town, one of the first to incorporate green 'wedges' of landscape. Photo: Frederick Gibberd. Photographer: Sam Lambert

Plate 11. Trees enhance new architecture in Cambridge. Photo: The Architectural Press. Photographer: Sam Lambert

Plate 12. One mature tree in the right position offers a dramatic and beautiful foil to the architecture in Oxford's High Street. Photo: The Architectural Press. Photographer: Sam Lambert

Plate 13. Planting along the pathway gives direction in Runcorn New Town. Photo: The Architectural Press

Plate 14. A spreading wych elm in a Durham cemetery acts as the focal point on the intersecting paths. Photo: Judy Cass

Plate 15. *Milton Keynes town centre trees soften the hard architecture, reduce solar glare and create smaller spaces out of the large square. Photo: The Architectural Press. Photographer: Peter Davey*

Plate 16. *Tree roots invading large brick-lined sewer (see p. 20). Photo: Reproduced by courtesy of the Manchester City Council*

Plates 17, 18. Trees reduce the scale of modern buildings and make the urban environment more acceptable. Imagine the view of St. Clement Danes in the Strand, London, without them. Photo: The Tree Council. Photographer: David Trace

Plate 19.   Crown renewal: a London plane allowed to re-grow a crown after drastic pollarding. Photo: Peter Bridgeman

Plate 20. Damage to lightly loaded boundary wall as result of growth of buttress roots (see p. 22)

Plate 21. Appearance of plane tree one year after heavy pruning (see p. 45)

Plate 22. Crown thinning: a trained and equipped professional removing crossing and weak branches to reduce density (see p. 53). Photo: Peter Bridgeman

Plate 23. Appearance of plane tree one year after light pruning (see p. 45)

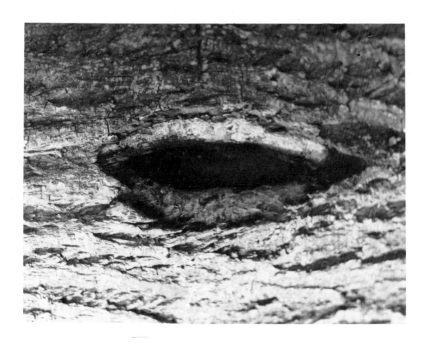

Plate 24. Bark wounds: one season's vigorous callus growth from the vertical sides of a cleaned and shaped bark wound (see p. 59). Photo: Peter Bridgeman

Plate 25. As above after one season's growth. Photo: Peter Bridgeman

Plate 26 (opposite). Reducing and shaping: a large oak growing close to house and road reduced to limit height and spread (see p. 54). Photo: Peter Bridgeman

Plate 27. Bracing equipment: eye bolts, screw eyes, cable, thimbles, bulldog grips and draw vice tensioner (see p. 62). Photo: Peter Bridgeman

Plate 28. Propping: a leaning catalpa propped with 5in. x 5in. timber and padded support (see p. 62). Photo: Peter Bridgeman

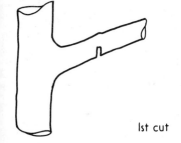

1st cut

Fig. 3.5. Branch removal, 1st cut: cutting up from under branch to prevent tearing

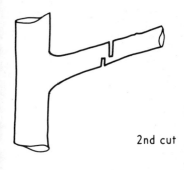

2nd cut

Fig. 3.6. Branch removal, 2nd cut: cutting down slightly further out but parallel to 1st cut. Branch will break cleanly along grain

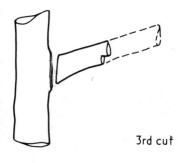

3rd cut

Fig. 3.7. Branch removal, 3rd cut: stump removed 'flush' to trunk, one cut from top

treated immediately with a tree paint. The function of a tree paint is to prevent the desiccation of the exposed living tissues and to form a barrier against airborne spores of wood-rotting fungi.

A range of tree paints is available but none, unfortunately, fulfils all the needs of a long-lasting protective false bark. Since the wound could take many years to heal over, the paint should be regularly re-applied.

Root pruning

Where roots of over 1in diameter are severed by trenching or reduction of soil levels around the tree, the root ends should be cut cleanly with a saw, painted with a tree paint and immediately covered with soil. If there is a risk of soil erosion through steep banks, a retaining wall should be constructed (see figure **3.8**).

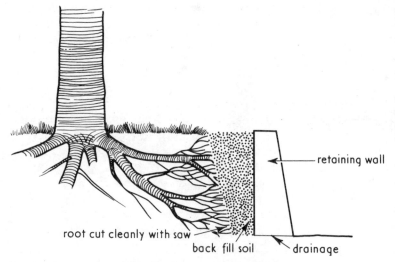

Fig. 3.8. Root pruning at retaining wall

REMEDIAL TREE SURGERY

Where trees have been damaged by man, animals pests or diseases, or storms, it is essential that the damaged area be treated as soon as possible to help the tree recover and prevent the invasion of wood-rotting fungi.

Superficial wounds are comparatively easy to treat but well-advanced areas of decay may be beyond control and the expense of the work must be justified against the value of the tree and its safety in relation to surrounding property.

Bark wounds

When areas of the protective bark have been damaged or removed, the wound should be cleaned by cutting back to sound wood and shaping the wound to encourage healing 'callus' growth. A 1½in or 2in carpenter's chisel and a mallet are used for the cutting and all damaged areas should be removed. Vertical wounds are easier to shape, as the callus growth will grow in from the sides (see Plate **24**). Horizontal wounds are more difficult, as there will be very little callus growth from the top and bottom of the wound. When such wounds have occurred, it is better to cut back to sound, undamaged wood and not make the wound any larger than necessary.

Many of the lower trunk wounds are caused by vehicles or grass-cutting equipment. Therefore, some form of protection should be erected or the grass kept clear of the trunk to prevent damage recurring.

Rots and cavities

Bark wounds, left untreated and old pruning cuts or damage caused by insects, animals and storms can give rise to rotting of the main heartwood of the trunk, branches or main anchor roots. Such rots are potentially very dangerous, as the tree's supportive strength will be reduced.

Rots which do not extend for more than 2in to 3in can be cleaned out with chisel and mallet. All obviously decayed and stained wood should be removed and the wound shaped as for bark wounds. The exposed wood should be treated with a thick dressing of tree paint. The wound should be checked every year, as the fungi causing the rot will still be present and further decay may be apparent.

Deeper cavities present more serious problems. It must first be determined whether the tree or branch is safe to retain, depending on its situation, and then to judge whether the cavity is worth the expense of cleaning and treating.

The safety of the tree and any recommended treatment can only be ascertained by an experienced arboriculturist. He will need to determine the extent of the rotten wood and this may entail opening up the access with a chain saw or purpose-made cavity cleaning tools. Alternatively, the extent of the rot can be judged by drilling into the trunk, above and below the obvious rot, with an auger.

The problem with opening up and drilling holes is the risk of spreading the rot from the heartwood into the active sapwood area of the trunk. Trees have the ability to form a barrier between the heartwood and sapwood to prevent the spread of rotting fungi. If the barrier is broken, the rots can extend, but, as

59

the important decision is to determine the tree's safety for surrounding property, it is often necessary to take the risk of spreading the rot.

Once the cavity has been opened, the obviously-rotten wood can be removed and this again, will help determine the safety of the tree. Accepting that all the disease organism cannot be removed, the cavity should be left open for re-inspection and further cleaning in the future.

Cavity filling can only hide the problem and make re-inspection more difficult. If it is necessary to hide the cavity for appearance's sake, it is better to cover with hessian or fine wire mesh rather than to fill.

Where cavities have developed deep water-holding pockets, again, the safety of the tree must be determined. Drilling up from below the rot with a large auger to drain the cavity could also help spread the rot from diseased heartwood to healthy sapwood and, therefore, is not recommended.

Extending the access hole down to the base of the water pocket may be necessary to determine the extent of the rot. If this is carried out, the exposed sapwood must be treated with a tree paint and regularly checked for signs of decay.

Some cavities can be strengthened by rod bracing (see cable bracing, page 61).

Storm damage
When branches have been blown out or splits have occurred during gales, it will be necessary to remove any broken branch stumps and paint the wounds.

Split trunks will require careful examination and in some instances can be supported by rod bracing.

Tree feeding
Trees growing in the unnatural conditions of tidy gardens and concrete cannot obtain the natural nutrients from decaying leaf-mould. It is not uncommon, therefore, to find trees in towns starved of the essential plant foods and some form of tree feeding may be required.

The type of manure or fertiliser to use and the method of application will depend on the surrounding soil conditions.

If there is open soil under the tree, a top-dressing of well rotted manure, compost or decomposed leaf-mould will help supply the nutrients and will prevent surface water evaporation.

Such materials are bulky and messy, and may not be acceptable. Therefore, compound granular fertiliser or liquid fertiliser may be required, especially where there is grass under the tree.

A slow-release compound is recommended and should be applied to the roots in the active growing season, i.e. March to July. To avoid surface loss, the fertiliser is best applied to pre-drilled holes around the rooting area of the tree. The holes are drilled at 2ft centres, 1ft deep, in a 10ft wide band around the branch-spread area.

Where the trees are growing in pavements or where there is no access to the root system, liquid fertilisers can be considered. The foliar sprays are useful for small trees but not very practical for large specimens.

PREVENTATIVE SURGERY

Trees may develop structural weaknesses which can, if recognised in time, be strengthened by cable or rod bracing, or by propping. If inserted correctly, the cables, rods or props prevent the occurrence of further damage.

Cable bracing

Many trees develop tight upward-growing forms or heavy horizontal branches which can easily split or break during winds.

One of the obsolete methods of preventing breakage was to secure a metal collar around the trunk and attach heavy solid rods or chains. This was ugly, very expensive and, since it did not allow for trunk expansion, soon caused constriction and damage.

The metal collars were replaced by slats of wood and the cable or chain passed round the trunk. This was better but still required regular maintenance and adjustment to prevent constriction.

Over the past twenty years, the method which has proven to be more satisfactory and quite inexpensive is to attach a flexible cable to eye-bolts or screw-eyes which are drilled through or into the trunks to be supported. The eye-bolt is inserted into a pre-drilled hole of the same diameter and secured with a diamond-shaped washer and nut on the back side of the branch. Screw-eyes are turned into holes drilled slightly smaller and are, therefore, cheaper to purchase and fix. The cable is secured to the eye of the bolt or screw with bulldog grips and a thimble is used to prevent chafing.

The positioning and angles of the cables are critical and should only be attempted by experienced staff.

Rod bracing

Although solid rods would create a too-rigid structure when supporting high branches, they can provide very effective support to areas of trunks or branches weakened by splitting or rots.

The rods are constructed from $\frac{1}{2}$in diameter mild steel and are threaded at both ends. A hole of the same diameter as the rod is drilled through the trunk and the rod secured in place with diamond washers and nuts (see Plate **27**).

Propping

Occasionally, it is not possible to secure with cables or rods, and low heavy branches, or even leaning trees, can be supported by propping from ground level.

Props constructed from wood or metal are placed on a concrete pad and positioned against the trunk or under the branch. Some form of protection for the trunk will be required (see Plate **28**).

Limitations of use

Although bracing and propping can prevent breakage, it must be carried out only by skilful staff and, even then, it does not guarantee that another branch on the same tree might not break.

The fact that the owner has admitted that the tree was insecure by carrying out bracing or propping could put him in an awkward situation if a person were injured or property damaged by a falling branch or tree.

Modern bracing requires, no maintenance, but regular checks should be made to see whether the original weakness is still sufficiently strong to support the branch or trunk.

FELLING

There are a number of statutes which control the unnecessary felling of trees but, because of disease or necessary building developments, or simply when trees are past the natural safe lifespan, they have to be removed. Tree felling in towns can provoke a great deal of controversy but, if there is planting of other trees to take the place of those felled, it should be part of the management plan.

If there is a good age-range of trees in the area, selective removal of old and weakened trees and replacement with young trees is often more cost-effective than tree surgery.

Methods of felling

Once it has been agreed that trees have to be felled, it is necessary to decide on the most appropriate method, depending on the size and position of the tree, and whether or not the stump and main roots are able to be removed.

Open-site felling

On large-scale clearance sites, trees are often pushed over by bulldozers, and the roots and branches burnt on site. If there is a number of trees, the timber may be worth a considerable amount of money.

Frequently, in towns, there is no access for large vehicles and felling has to be carried out by felling to ground level with chain-saws and removing the stump with hand-winches.

Where there are no surrounding hazards, the feller will decide on the direction of fall, taking into account the natural weight of the tree and how to facilitate easy removal of the timber and branches. Once the direction has been determined, a wedge of wood is cut out of the base of the trunk in line with the intended direction of fall (see figure **3.9**). The position of the wedge, or 'sink', is critical and a great deal of experience is required to make the cuts accurately. The tree is felled by cutting through the trunk from the opposite side to the sink. This back-cut must never be lower than the base of the sink and is often made slightly higher (see figure **3.10**).

If the tree does not have a naturally heavy side, the initial momentum in line with the intended direction of fall is assisted by driving a wedge into the back-cut or by attaching a pull-rope or winch-cable higher in the tree before the sink is cut.

Once the tree has fallen, the side branches are cut and removed. The main trunk may have timber value but, if there is no access for vehicles, it is often necessary to cut the trunk into small easily-handled sections for disposal.

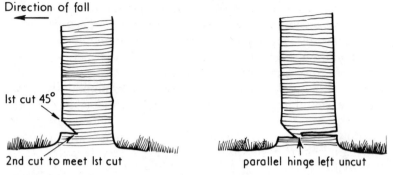

Direction of fall

1st cut 45°

2nd cut to meet 1st cut

parallel hinge left uncut

Fig. 3.9. (left) Tree felling by chain-saw: wedge or 'sink' of wood removed

Fig. 3.10. Tree felling by chain-saw: back-severing cut, slightly higher than base of 'sink'

Felling in confined situations

Due to the presence of surrounding features such as buildings, roads and underground or overhead services, it is often impossible to fell the tree from ground level. In such situations, the entire crown may have to be lowered to the ground with ropes or, with very large difficult trees, a crane.

Lowering heavy branches and trunks with ropes, and handling chain-saws at height, is potentially very dangerous and should only be attempted by experienced staff.

In confined situations, it is often impossible for lorries to drive close enough for removal of large timber and this type of work can be very labour-intensive and, therefore, expensive.

The use of cranes which can lift timber over obstructions is often necessary.

Stump removal

It is not normally necessary to remove all the tree's roots but the stump and major anchor roots will often have to be excavated for replanting or building.

If the tree has been cut off to ground level, there are several methods of removing the remaining stump. Hand-digging is a very slow, laborious method and is only practicable with small trees or, sometimes, in pavements where machinery cannot be used. Hand-winches are very efficient tools to aid stump removal as long as there is a strong anchor. Care must be taken, however, if there are nearby underground services. A hand-operated tree jack is commonly used for pushing out small trees in pavements.

The above methods are satisfactory where there is limited access but are expensive on labour. A number of firms have stump-cutting machines available for hire, with operator. These are either tractor-mounted or towed by a Land-Rover or similar vehicle. The smallest machine requires a minimum access of 4ft. and the very large stump cutters, which can tackle even the largest stumps, require access of at least 8ft. The machines can cut down into the soil at least 2ft, thus reducing all the stump and main roots to easily-handled chippings (see Plate **29**).

Blasting stumps with explosives is practised on large, open sites but only by fully licensed and experienced professionals.

If the stumps can be left in situ the re-growth problem can be reduced by applying total weed-killers to the stump, such as ammonium sulphamate or sodium chlorate.

Brushwood disposal
The disposal of branches and twigs from pruning or felling operations can be a serious problem in towns. Burning is often prohibited and the tipping of bulky loose brushwood is not normally allowed at council refuse tips.

Transporting brushwood out of town is very expensive on lorries and labour and, if a local authority or large contractor has a disposal problem, it can be overcome by using a brushwood-chipping machine (see Plate **30**). These machines reduce the brushwood and trunks up to 8in diameter to 1/15th of their bulk by chipping them into small fragments. The resulting chippings can be tipped or, if properly decomposed and disease-free, used as mulching material.

LABOUR REQUIREMENTS

Most of the operations mentioned require staff with considerable expertise if the tree is to be maintained properly and surrounding features protected. The work is arduous and potentially very dangerous. Therefore, only skilled, properly trained and equipped staff should be employed.

Local authorities and large land-owners have the choice of engaging their own staff for the work or employing contractors.

DIRECT LABOUR

Having your own labour-force for tree-work has many

advantages. They will always be available for regular maintenance operations and in the event of emergencies. You have control over the selection, training and equipping of the staff and can plan the work systematically over the seasons.

Smaller authorities and garden owners, however, would not always have sufficient work to justify a permanent team and, with the responsibilities of safety and supervision, employ specialist contractors.

If it is decided to employ direct labour, it is essential to consider the proper selection, training, equipping and supervision of the staff.

Selection
Staff for tree-work must be physically fit and able to work at height. These essential qualities can be determined by medical examination and by work experience. If any staff do not meet the standards, they should be found less arduous employment. It is possible to engage trained staff, as more training and educational courses are now available.

Training
It is fundamental that all staff be trained to a safe and competent level. Even the most mundane of tasks, such as clearing branches, loading lorries and fire-lighting, require considerable expertise and should not be left to untrained recruits.

A training and work-experience plan should be prepared for the staff, including all the operations they will be asked to perform.

A number of educational establishments offer training courses in tree-work operations and validated schemes of training are organised by the Local Government Training Board (see Local Government Training Recommendations for Parks and Playing Fields Employees, available from L.G.T.B., 8 The Arndale Centre, Luton, LU1 2TS). The City & Guilds of London Institute offer an Arboricultural Practice option at the Stage II level, and their 014 Certificate in Arboriculture assesses both theoretical knowledge and practical skills. Further details are obtainable from City & Guilds, 46 Britannia Street, London, WC1X 9RG.

Full-time courses leading to the National Certificate in Horticulture (Arboriculture) and the Ordinary National Diploma in Arboriculture are available at Merrist Wood

Agricultural College, Worplesdon, nr. Guildford, Surrey.

Short practical training courses in safe and efficient tree work are offered by Honey Bros. (Sales) Ltd. in conjunction with Peter Bridgeman & Associates. These courses can be planned at the employer's own premises. Details are obtainable from Honey Bros. (Sales) Ltd., Peasmarsh, Guildford, Surrey or Peter Bridgeman & Associates, 20 Wood Street, Ash Vale, nr. Aldershot, Hants.

Equipment

If staff are to be able to carry out all the operations mentioned in this chapter, they will require a considerable amount of machinery and equipment.

Safety climbing equipment and protective clothing are essential, as are all the necessary hand-tools, ropes, chain-saws and hand-winches. For larger felling operations, power-winches and heavy lifting equipment will be required. Larger employers may also require hydraulic platforms, brushwood chippers and stump-cutting machines.

Transport will be required, unless the staff are full-time, engaged in one park.

Supervision

However well-trained and equipped the staff are, they will require regular supervision to ensure standards of work and safety. The supervisor will need to know the practicalities of the work and be able to control staff effectively.

Many authorities have incentive bonus schemes and, if these are to work efficiently and safely, the supervisor must plan, co-ordinate and check all work.

CONTRACTORS

Due to the cost and expertise of establishing and supervising direct labour teams, many will employ contractors for their tree-work operations. This has many advantages but finding contractors of the required calibre is not always easy in some parts of the country. Anybody can buy a chain-saw and van, and call himself a 'tree surgeon'. To the unsuspecting, this could prove disastrous and the employer of contractors could still be responsible for public safety.

It is essential, therefore, to employ only experienced, fully-insured contractors. The reputation and standards of local firms may be known but, if not known, it is best to employ only 'approved companies'. The Arboricultural Association issues a free list of approved firms, available from The Secretary, Brokerswood House, Brokerswood, Westbury, Wilts.

Many authorities compromise between direct labour and contractor by having a small well-trained and equipped labour team for regular maintenance work and on call for emergencies, and employing contractors for the large-scale operations and where expensive specialist machinery is required.

When employing contractors, it is advisable to obtain at least two or three quotations for the work and, to ensure that all are pricing on the same basis, a detailed specification and contract document may be required.

The specification should clearly state all the required work and clarify such details as disposal of timber and branches, whether or not fires are permitted, etc. Contractors should be supervised to ensure that the work is carried out in accordance with the specification.

4

Tree diseases and disorders

David Burdekin

The presence of trees in our urban streets and open spaces helps to soften the harsher man-made landscape: green foliage in summer, the autumn colour and the tracery of the winter branches contrast with the solid shapes of buildings and roads. However, when trees in urban situations become diseased, their value to the landscape is lost. There is premature loss of leaves and the decayed or dead tree is a danger to surrounding buildings and to passing motorists or pedestrians.

Trees, like human beings, do not become unhealthy without reason. In some cases, trees are attacked by infectious diseases, usually caused by microscopic organisms called fungi or bacteria. Such diseases are often specific to one type of tree though, sometimes, they can affect a wide range of host trees. In other cases, trees may be affected by deleterious environmental factors, such as pollution or even vandalism.

The best-known tree disease is Dutch elm disease, a devastating affliction of elms which, by the end of 1978, had destroyed nearly two-thirds of the elm population of southern Britain. This disease has had a particularly dramatic effect on rural areas where the English elm was predominant in the landscape. But its effects have been equally severe in many urban areas where elm was grown. Impressive avenues of Wheatley elm, the conical, almost Christmas-tree-shaped elm have been killed in most major cities in southern Britain. In many recent urban developments, English elms in old hedgerows have been retained and incorporated as street trees. A particularly good example was in Basildon New Town in Essex, where Dutch elm disease destroyed a large proportion of the mature tree population in the early 1970s, leaving the town almost bereft of trees.

However, it would be quite wrong to give the impression that all tree diseases are as serious as Dutch elm disease. It is almost certainly the most serious disease of ornamental trees in Europe and North America. Many other tree diseases are relatively insignificant but some are, of course, damaging and it is important that these are recognised and dealt with in an appropriate manner.

In this chapter, the diseases selected for detailed consideration (see table 4.1) include those found on tree species commonly planted in towns. The wide variety of symptoms caused by disease in different parts of a tree, including the crown,

Table 4.1 Common diseases of urban trees

Disease	Casual agent	Tree
Anthracnose	*Gnomonia platani*	*Platanus* spp. (planes)
Anthracnose	*Marssonina salicicola*	*Salix* spp. (willows)
Bacterial canker	*Xanthomonas populi*	*Populus* spp. (poplars)
Fire blight	*Erwinia amylovora*	*Crataegus* spp. (especially red hawthorns) *Sorbus aria* (whitebeam)
Dutch elm disease	*Ceratocystis ulmi*	*Ulmus* spp. (elms)
Beech bark disease	*Nectria coccinea*	*Fagus sylvatica* (beech)
Decay	*Wide range of decay fungi*	Most woody plants
Honey fungus	*Armillaria mellea*	All woody plants
Phytophthora root rot	*Phytophthora* spp.	Many woody plants

branches, stem or roots, are well illustrated by these examples. Other tree diseases, either of lesser importance or on trees less frequently found in towns, are not mentioned here and the interested reader should consult the list of references given at the end of this chapter for further reading. Special mention is made of oak wilt at the end of the section on tree diseases. This is a serious disease of oak, present in North America, but not recorded in Britain.

Methods for the treatment of diseased trees are discussed in most cases but it is clear from the examples given that eradication of disease is often very difficult. Preventative measures, such as careful choice and preparation of planting site and the use of resistant varieties, are often, though not always, more important than curative treatments. The use of a range of different tree species can help to reduce the effects of losses from disease. From this point of view, the wide-scale use of elms in some of our cities in the past may serve as a salutary lesson. It is also important to recognise that, in some circumstances, remedial treatments may not be necessary and the tree may recover from a temporary set-back.

Disorders of trees caused by a range of adverse environmental agents can be confused with genuine tree diseases. Pollution of the air by toxic fumes is one of the commonest causes. Although it is often difficult to prove that air pollution is responsible for damage, there is a growing volume of information to help in the identification of pollution damage. A list of the more important agents responsible for environmental damage to trees is given in table 4.2 and a description of symptoms and their related causes is given later in this chapter.

Table 4.2   Common disorders of urban trees

Causal agent	Trees
Air pollution	
sulphur dioxide	Many woody plants
fluoride	Many woody plants
Man	
physical damage	Most woody plants
soil or root disturbance	Most woody plants

TREE DISEASES

Anthracnose of London plane

London plane is probably one of the most widely planted tree species in urban areas in Britain and any disease which occurs on it clearly warrants close attention. The most common disease of London plane is an anthracnose (a type of plant disease where

71

discrete spots of diseased tissue develop on both leaves and stems), caused by the fungus usually called *gnomonia platani* though other names are sometimes used. See Plate **31**.

It was first recorded in England in 1810 and was particularly serious on the Occidental plane (*platanus occidentalis*), a species now uncommon in this is country, perhaps because of repeated attacks by *g. platani*. However, London plane (*platanus* X *acerifolia*), a hybrid between the Oriental plane (*platanus orientalis*) and the Occidental plane, is generally more resistant. Normally, it causes little damager but, when climatic conditions are particularly favourable for its development, spectacular symptoms can be seen. The last serious outbreak occurred in early summer 1979, following a particularly cold winter and cool, moist spring.

The fungus cause s four separate forms of damage:

Bud blight. The fungus winters in the bud, invading and killing the tissues so that the bud does not open in the spring. Frequently, the fungus grows into the adjacent twig, killing the bark and cambium for a few centimetres above and below the bud. If the stem is not girdled, and this is often the case, a small oval canker develops at the infected node.

Twig blight. This occurs when the fungus from an infected bud invades the stem, girdling it and thereby causing the distal portion to die back. Sometimes, infection may spread down from a terminal bud to cause a tip die-back. Twig blight may also occur when a twig is girdled following an attack during the next phase, shoot blight.

Shoot blight. Shoot blight is perhaps the most spectacular form of the disease. Young developing shoots, from 1 to as much as 10 centimeters long, wilt and die. The whole shoot turns yellow or brown and the leaves are subsequently shed. These symptoms may occur in parts of the crown or distributed throughout the tree. In extreme cases, where the whole tree is affected soon after flushing, it may be entirely leafless for a period. Attacks which develop a few weeks later cause a generally discoloured crown and the ground below may be littered with fallen leaves, giving the appearance of a premature autumn.

Leaf blight Distinct symptoms start to appear on the leaves in early summer. Brown, dead patches develop on either side of the leaf veins which, themslelves, become clearly outlined in black. The dead patches vary in size from 1 to 5 centrimetres across and can be found on almost any part of the leaf and, in extreme cases, they appear along all the main veins and down into the petiole.

The overall effect of these symptoms may be particularly dramatic in the spring when dead, brown leaves may be observed throughout the crown of the tree and parts, at least, of the crown may fail to flush.

Local spread of this disease is by means of fungal spores carried in rain splash. In addition, however, another type of spore is produced on fallen infected leaves: these are wind-borne and can spread the disease over long distances.

Control is normally impracticable and, in any case, usually unnecessary. Although the effect of the disease may be dramatic in the spring, a further flush of disease-free leaves usually occurs during the summer and the affected trees normally recover in the same or in the following season.

A number of clones of London plane have been planted over the past one or two hundred years and some variation in their susceptibility to anthracnose has been observed. It is possible , by careful observation and testing, that a resistant clone or clones could be selected.

Anthracnose of weeping willow
A second anthracnose disease giving rise to concern is that on weeping willow Plate **32.** This is caused by the fungus *marssonina salicicola*. It was first reported in Britain in 1930 on the basket willow *salix purpurea*. It was not until the 1960s that the disease was commonly reported on weeping willow (variously known as *salix x chrysocoma, S. alba 'vitellina' x babylonica, s. alba 'vitellina pendula', S. alba 'tristis'* and *s. babylonica 'ramulis aureis'*). It has also been found infrenquently on other willow species.

Small brown or purplish spots, some 2 to 4 mm across and circular or elliptical in shape, develop on the leaves and current year's shoots. The symptoms appear in early spring, as the new growth is starting, and infection can cause distortion and death of the leaves and young shoots. Later in the season, the spots on the shoots develop into small rough cankers which can persist for several years. When the tree is severely attacked, it may lose a large proportion of the developing foliage and the crown appears thin and untidy. Later in the season, new growth of pendulous shoots occurs and the tree often regains its characteristic appearance but, on occasion, recovery may be far from complete.

The microscopic asexual spores of the causal fungus can sometimes be seen en masse as a white speck in the centre of the leaf

73

spot. They are probably spread largely by rain splash. Successful infection is largely idependent on the presence of moisture for the production and dispersal of spores and particularly serious attacks occur after periods of high moisture. It is not surprising, therefore, that the disease is prevalent during a damp spring or early summer.

The disease can be controlled by the use of preventative fungicides: once infection has become established, it cannot be eliminated. The use of sprays on large trees clearly present practical problems but treatment of smaller specimens should be possible. In trials conducted in the late 1960s, it was established that sprays in the first and third week in May gave good control but it may be necessary to continue with further fortnightly treatments if wet or humid conditions persist into June. The fungicide, benomyl, should give effective control, applied at the rates recommended for black spot of roses.

Poplar canker

Poplar canker is caused by the bacterium *xanthomonas populi* and it is one of only a few diseases of trees caused by bacteria. On a susceptible species or cultivar of poplar, this disease causes serious die-back ands, sometimes, death of trees. See Plate **33.**

The characteristic symptom of poplar canker is a cankerous outgrowth on the main stem or branch, which can vary greatly in size, shape and surface texture. For example, cankers may be large outgrowths some 30 cm or more across, with a rough surface, or much smaller and smooth-surfaced. However, the first symptom to develop is often on the one-year-old shoot, close to the leaf scar. A crack forms just below the bud and, in very moist conditions, a cream-coloured slime is exuded. The twig my be girdled, in which case it dies or, alternatively, a perennial canker may develop over the course of several years. Sometimes, an elongated canker or series of cankers may be found on a stem and these appear to be associated with a tunnel below the bark made by an insect, the poplar cambial miner. The bacteria seem able to travel down this tunnel and cause erumpent cankers at intervals down the stem. There is no evidence that insects, such as the cambial miner mentioned above, are responsible for the spread of the disease from tree to tree, though this is, nevertheless, possible. It is much more likely that the bacteria are spread by rain falling on the bacterial exudate and subsequent splashing of bacteria to freshly exposed leaf scars and other infection sites.

The best method of control is the use of resistant clones. Many of the older balsam poplars planted in Britain proved very susceptible to bacterial canker and, as a result, the whole group of clones of *Populus trichocarpa* gained a bad reputation for susceptibility. More recent screening of cultivars, however, has shown a high resistance in members of this group, including the cultivars 'Scott Pauley' and 'Fritzi Pauley'. Members of the Italian black hybrid poplars are often used in Europe for roadside plantings and care is taken to select resistant clones for planting where the disease is known to occur. One of the most resistant cultivars grown in Britain is the Lombardy poplar, *P. nigra* 'italica'.

Fire blight

Fire blight (Plate **34**) was first reported in England in the late 1950s, when it was found attacking pear trees in the south-east of the country. It is a second example of a tree disease caused by a bacterium, in this case *Erwinia amylovora*. In addition to pears, this bacterium can also infect many woody and herbaceous members of the rose family (*Rosaceae*). Amongst tree species which are commonly attacked are the cultivated red hawthorns (*Crataegus oxyacantha*), the wild hawthorns (*Crataegus monogyna*) and whitebeam (*Sorbus aria*). It has also been found on mountain ash (*Sorbus aucuparia*).

One of the first signs of fire blight in the spring is the wilting of young foliage, shoots and flowers. Affected parts rapidly turn brown or black and give the impression of having been scorched by fire. In warm, wet weather, droplets of slimy, milky fluid containing very large numbers of infectious bacteria may exude from the diseased blossoms or shoots. The bacteria may also move down within the stem to larger branches below and kill them: sometimes, the whole tree may be killed. The colour of the bark becomes darker as the infection spreads through the stem beneath and the inner bark is first water-soaked and then turns reddish brown.

In the autumn, the bacteria usually cease spreading and cracks may appear at the edge of areas of infected bark and a canker may develop. Bacteria survive the winter in these cankered areas and, during the following spring, a bacterial slime, similar to that found on the young shoots, may exude from their surface.

A number of insects, including bees, flies and ants, are attracted to the bacterial slime which exudes in the spring from the wintering cankers. The bacteria are carried on the bodies of the insects. If they subsequently visit flowers of a susceptible species, the bacteria can be transmitted to, and infect, the new season's growth. The disease can also be spread by insects to wounds on the tree or by man through the use of contaminated pruning implements.

This disease can be controlled, provided infection is not widespread in the tree, by pruning off affected parts. Infected branches should be cut at least 45 cm below the area where the bark is discoloured. Pruning tools must be disinfected between all cuts to ensure that infection is not spread to the clean surfaces. Most household disinfectants should be effective, though some may corrode the tools if they are not washed and dried after use.

Where infection has spread to within 60 cm or so of the main trunk, it is unlikely that the tree will survive. In this case, the tree should be felled and all the wood should be burnt. If possible, the root system should also be removed or, if this is not practicable, the stump should be treated (according to the manufacturer's instructions) with a chemical such as ammonium sulphate, in order to prevent re-growth of infected shoots.

If fire blight is known to be present in an area and causing serious damage, it is unwise to plant susceptible trees. Members of the *Rosaceae* family should perhaps be avoided or only relatively resistant species, such as *Sorbus intermedia,* should be planted.

Dutch elm disease

The recent history of Dutch elm disease (Plate **35**) is familiar to many, particularly those in southern Britain, where two-thirds of the original elm population had been destroyed by the end of 1978. However, it is sometimes forgotten that the disease has been present in Britain for more than 50 years and in Europe for even longer. It was first identified in Europe in 1918 in Picardy, France, and the first report in Britain was on an elm near a golf course at Totteridge, Hertfordshire, in 1927. During the 1930s, a widespread epidemic occurred and it has been estimated that 10 to 15 per cent of the British elm population was killed during that period. The epidemic declined in the 1940s and there were only periodic local 'flare-ups' of the disease until the start of the current epidemic in the late 1960s.

The characteristic symptoms appear from June onwards and include a wilting of the leaves over a part, or sometimes the whole, of the tree, soon followed by yellowing and loss of foliage. Quite frequently, the wilted leaves turn brown and remain attached to the tree for some time. The fast-growing shoots may also wilt and their tips turn downwards as they die, to form miniature 'shepherd's crooks'. When an elm is severely attacked, the entire tree may be dead before the end of the season. In some cases, it may survive only to die the following spring, as a result of infection spreading down from one year's growth into the next.

If infected twigs are cut with a sharp knife or pair of secateurs, they often show a ring of small dark brown spots in the outermost parts of the wood. A similar staining in the form of longitudinal streaks can be seen if the bark is peeled away and the wood gently shaved. These markings are not always found but, if present, they provide a useful diagnostic characteristic.

Much of the early research into the biology of Dutch elm disease was undertaken by European scientists, especially the Dutch – hence the name of the disease. It was found that the disease is caused by a fungus now known as *Ceratocystis ulmi*. The fungus infects the vascular system of the tree and either blocks or poisons the sap stream. This fungus was again under intensive study in the early 1970s and, in 1973, it was discovered that the recent outbreak of Dutch elm disease was caused by a new and hitherto unsuspected strain of *C. ulmi*. The so-called 'aggressive' strain was probably introduced into Britain on rock elm logs imported from Canada.

In Britain, the fungus is transmitted from diseased to healthy trees by two species of bark beetle, *Scolytus scolytus* and *Scolytus multistriatus*. Both beetle species have a shiny black thorax (the area in front of the wings) and dark red-brown wing cases. *S. scolytus* is 5 to 6 mm long whereas *S. multistriatus* is only 2.5 to 3.5 mm long. These beetles breed in the bark of dead or dying elms and the developing larvae produce characteristic gallery systems in the inner bark (see Plate **36**). The larvae pupate in the bark and emerge in the spring or summer carrying spores of the fungus, which have formed in the insect galleries. In order to complete the infection cycle, adult beetles feed in the crotches between small twigs of a healthy elm and introduce fungal spores

77

into the vascular system of the tree. The healthy elm is thereby infected and the fungus spreads through the tree, causing the disease symptoms to develop. In addition to transmission by the beetle, the fungus can also spread from tree to tree through connecting roots. This commonly occurs in hedgerows of English Elm, where many trunks are supported by a common root system, but it also occurs when the roots of neighbouring trees are grafted to one another.

The basis of control programmes against Dutch elm disease is sanitation felling i.e. the felling of all diseased elms and the destruction of the bark. In this way, the breeding grounds for the beetle are destroyed and the adult beetles are prevented from emerging to spread the disease to neighbouring healthy trees. Such programmes cannot be expected to eradicate the disease but they have been shown in many cases to reduce markedly the rate of disease progress.

Where there is the danger of disease transmission through the roots, steps should be taken to prevent this. The roots connecting neighbouring trees can either be severed mechanically or killed with a suitable chemical so that the fungus is unable to move from diseased to healthy trees.

Many attempts have been made to develop effective chemical control measures to combat the disease. A variety of chemicals has been tested, either against the carrier beetles or against the fungus. Insecticides have been sprayed on to healthy trees in order to protect them against attack by the bark beetles. Amongst the first to be used in experiments in the United States was DDT and, although it proved to be at least partially effective, its use is not longer permitted. An alternative and safer chemical, methoxychlor, was introduced later but the application of insecticidal sprays to large urban trees has proved difficult, expensive and unacceptable in most urban environments. More recently, research has concentrated on the possible use of natural attractants, called pheromones. These pheromones can be used as a bait in insect traps but their potential for use in control programmes seems to be rather limited at this stage.

The use of fungicides has also been under investigation but the application technique is different. It has involved the injection, under pressure, of a fungicidal solution into the trunk or roots of a healthy elm, in order to prevent the fungus from infecting the tree. However, fungicidal injection is an expensive treatment which must be repeated annually for several years and it offers no guarantee of success.

None of the chemical treatments mentioned above can be expected on its own to make a significant impact on the disease and it should only be used in conjunction with sanitation felling, in order to improve the effectiveness of an overall programme.

In the longer term, the possibility of selecting or breeding elms resistant to the disease seems a promising approach. A number of Asiatic elms, including selections from *Ulmus pumila* (the Siberian elm) and *Ulmus japonica* (the Japanese elm), have shown marked resistance to Dutch elm disease. For a number of years, European and North American scientists have been selecting and testing a range of elm material, including some with Asiatic elms in their parentage. Several resistant cultivars have been released to the nursery trade in Holland and North America for pilot-scale plantings. Such trials will not only enable scientists to confirm the resistance of these cultivars in the field but also provide an opportunity to assess the trees' ability to withstand a range of climatic and soil conditions. In addition, observations on the form and vigour of these cultivars will be made, in order to provide information on the most suitable situations for planting. Two cultivars currently under test in the United States are the urban elm and Sapporo Autumn Gold, both of which are likely to be more suitable for urban planting. These and other resistant elms will be tested in Britain over the next few years.

Beech bark disease
Beech bark disease is perhaps one of the best-known stem diseases of trees. Despite the fact that it has been present in Britain for over a century, it has been heralded in some quarters as the successor to Dutch elm disease. The evidence that has been accumulated over a long period indicates that beech bark disease can cause death of valuable large beech trees and be responsible for severe local outbreaks in plantations – but is not likely to be a national epidemic.

Beech bark disease is caused by the combined attack of two organisms, the beech scale insect (*Cryptococcus fagisuga*) and a fungus (*Nectria coccinea*). The beech scale insect, also known as the
most of its life-cycle living in colonies on beech bark. It is largely sedentary and is covered with a white, waxy protective wool.

When the main trunk of a beech tree becomes heavily infested, it has the appearance of being white-washed.

The coccus does not act as a vector nor does it, alone, cause the disease. However, over a period of time, it weakens the bark so that the fungus can infect the inner bark regions. Patches of dead bark develop on the main stem or branches of beech and separate infections often coalesce to produce large vertical strips of dead bark or girdling of the stem (or both).

One of the most striking symptoms of beech bark disease is the presence of blackish spots, 2 cm or more in diameter, on the bark surface. These so-called 'tarry spots' often exude a sticky liquid. Each tarry spot is the centre of a patch of dead bark and this can be demonstrated by exposing, with a knife cut, the orange-brown-coloured tissue beneath the bark surface. At a later stage, the tiny pinkish-red fruit bodies of *N. coccinea* (1 mm or less in diameter) may emerge through the surface of bark killed by the fungus.

Once the stem or branch has been girdled, the whole tree or the distal portions of the affected limbs will die. In some cases, this may be preceded by the presence of yellowing or sparse foliage but this does not always occur and such symptoms can be produced from other causes. Once the bark has been killed by the disease, ambrosia beetles can bore into the wood below and introduce wood-rotting fungi. These fungi cause a rapid deterioration of the woody tissues and the rotted stems are liable to break. Such breakage is known as 'beech snap' and usually occurs on badly-affected trees up to a height of about 5 metres.

This disease has proved extremely difficult to control, though infestations of the coccus can be treated and killed with insecticides, such as diazinon. It is also possible that surgical treatment of the bark surrounding tarry spots, and treatment with a fungicide, may help to eradicate the fungus. However, further research is required before the effectiveness of this treatment can be fully assessed.

The deaths of large numbers of mature beech trees have been reported from many parts of Britain in recent years and there has been some speculation that beech bark disease may have been responsible. However, reports were particularly numerous following the drought years of 1975 and 1976. Many trees on sandy or limestone soils, where drought conditions were especially severe, died as a consequence of the drought. Others were previously weakened by other agents, such as root disease or even old age, and they finally died, with the extra stress caused by drought. In many areas, trees were observed which exhibited the tarry spot symptoms previously described for beech bark disease but in the absence of the beech coccus. It appears, in these instances, that the drought had in some way weakened the tree and allowed fungal infection of bark.

Decay
Decay takes many years to develop in living trees and, because affected trees often remain apparently healthy, its presence is often difficult to detect. Indeed, extensive rot in trees may only become evident after a branch or stem has broken or the whole tree is uprooted (Plate 37). By this time, severe damage may have been done to neighbouring buildings, vehicles or passers-by. It is clearly important for those concerned with the care of trees to be aware of the recognisable and outward signs of decay, and to take appropriate action where necessary. This applies particularly to the trained arboriculturist, who may have responsibilities for large numbers of trees but also to the individual with a large tree in his garden which is growing close to roads or buildings. If the presence of decay is suspected, an expert should be called upon without delay to examine the suspect tree.

Decay can be caused by a large number of different fungi: some decay fungi attack only a limited range of tree species, others are more wide-ranging. In all cases, microscopic threads of the fungus, called hyphae, invade the woody tissues and feed on the lignin or cellulose, the major structural components of wood. The strength of the wood is thereby weakened and it becomes increasingly liable to fracture. Breakage of stems, branches or roots is most common during high winds but can also occur during relatively still conditions, when the weight of the limb is too great to be supported by the decayed wood.

Decay fungi can enter a tree through the branches, trunk or roots. Above ground the most common places of entry are pruning wounds, areas of mechanical damage on the trunk and wounds left by natural breakage of branches: entry through the intact bark is uncommon. Below ground, however, there is a number of decay fungi which can infect undamaged roots, though information on the biology of many root-decay fungi is very limited.

81

Like most other fungi, those causing decay produce fruit bodies in which the spores or seeds of the fungus develop. These spores provide the common means by which the fungus is dispersed to infect other trees. Most decay fungi produce fruit bodies in the general form of mushrooms or toadstools. Many do not have a stalk but are directly attached to the trunk of the tree in the form of a bracket.

There are twenty or more fungi which commonly cause decay in trees and the interested student must refer to an authoritative text for detailed information. Two examples will be briefly described here, one, a fungus causing stem decay and the other, one causing a root rot.

Inonotus hispidus is very commonly found on ash, particularly following pruning. The fruit body is often produced on the main trunk, somewhat above or below the pruning wound. It first appears in May or June as a rusty-coloured semicircular bracket, ranging in size from 6 to 35 cm across and 2 to 10 cm deep. The upper surface is covered with short bristles (technically called 'hispid', hence the specific name) and the lower surface consists of minute pores. Within a month or so, the fruit body turns black and has the texture of loose charcoal. It eventually falls to the ground during the winter months.

Decay is usually found in the heartwood of infected trees and advanced decay is yellowish-green in colour and spongy in texture. The decayed zone is surrounded in cross section by a narrow, brown, gummy band of tissue. Decay by this fungus rapidly weakens the wood and, even before its presence in the wood can be detected by eye, there is a rapid deterioration in some of the strength properties of the wood.

Meripilus giganteus, on the other hand, is a root-decay fungus, commonly found on beech and is rarely found above ground. Extensive decay in the root systems often occurs before the fruit body appears. The presence of the fruit body is, therefore, important and acts as a warning that the tree is in serious danger of being blown over.

As the specific name of *M. giganteus* suggests, the fruit body is very large. It consists of a mass of overlapping fronds which, overall, may be more than 60 cm across. It develops at the base of the main trunk or on the ground nearby. The upper surface is brownish-yellow, often darkening to chestnut-brown. The creamy-white lower surface is covered with minute pores. The fruit body usually develops between July and September, and rapidly deteriorates into a black slimy mass following the first severe autumn frosts.

The decay in the roots is generally brown in colour and, at an advanced stage, the roots and stump become completely hollow. In some cases, root decay may be so extensive that signs of ill-health are apparent in the crown of the tree, for example, leaves may become yellow prematurely or the whole crown may be sparsely foliated.

The presence of fruit bodies of decay fungi is one of the most valuable indicators of the presence of decay in a tree. An expert should always be called upon to give advice in such circumstances. The appearance of such fruit bodies should be taken as a warning about the tree's safety but care must be taken to ensure that the fruit body is of a fungus which causes decay. This is particularly important in the case of fruit bodies found at the base of the tree, for many found in that situation are harmless or even beneficial.

There are other useful indicators of the presence of decay. In the presence of *M. giganteus,* it was mentioned that the whole crown of the tree may be affected and this may occur with other root-decay fungi. There are, however, other factors which can produce similar effects and such symptoms are not diagnostic of decay.

Above ground, wounds of various types are the most likely entry points for decay. They should be examined carefully and binoculars used, if necessary, to see if any signs of decay are present. Another place where decay often develops is in the crotch between acutely-angled stems. Inconspicuous splits may be present, indicating that there is a danger of the limbs splitting apart. Another potential danger spot is where branches or stems have developed with right-angled bends, perhaps because the original axis has been lost by death or breakage.

It would, of course, be much more desirable to prevent the initial entry of decay and, thereby, avoid the careful inspection and other measures required later. Treatments are often applied routinely to pruning wounds in order to keep out decay organisms and to encourage the healing over of wounds by the growth of callus tissues. However, such treatments have met with mixed success and it is not unusual to find decay developing behind the treated surface. Research is currently being undertaken in this country and the United States to improve the effectiveness of pruning-wound treatments. Nevertheless, it is still too early to recommend a treatment which can both prevent decay and stimulate healing.

Honey fungus

The commonest root disease of trees in Britain is that caused by honey fungus (*Armillaria mellea*). It is particularly common in areas which have previously been characterised by broadleaved woodlands or old hedgerows and it takes a steady toll of trees or woody ornamentals planted in such areas. Trees in parks or gardens with a previous history of woodland are, therefore, more likely to be affected than roadside trees.

Within a relatively small area and over a period of years, honey fungus is likely to kill one or two plants each year. It does not cause large numbers of deaths in a short time. The death of individuals may be sudden or may follow a gradual die-back.

Death of trees in this manner is not alone, of course, sufficient to diagnose honey fungus as the cause. One of the best diagnostic features of this disease is the presence of a creamy-white fungal skin beneath the bark at the base of the tree. This symptom can be detected by taking a sharp knife and cutting through the bark at the root collar region and exposing the wood below.

In addition to causing death of trees and shrubs, honey fungus can cause decay in the root system, rendering trees liable to uprooting. This decay rarely extends more than a metre or so up the stem.

Dead trees or stumps, and their associated root systems, can act as the source from which honey fungus spreads to neighbouring live trees. It is able to survive for decades in large stumps and it spreads out into the surrounding soil by means of thin black strands known as rhizomorphs or, more popularly, as 'bootlaces'. These rhizomorphs can grow for many metres from their source and, when a rhizomorph tip encounters a live root, it can pierce and kill the bark. Whitish sheets of fungal material form and spread beneath the bark, killing the live parts of the root. At the same time, the fungus grows into the woody tissues of the root, causing decay. It slowly invades the whole root system of the tree and, once it reaches the collar region at the base of the main stem, the tree is likely to be girdled and killed. At this stage, the whitish sheets formed by the fungus may be present beneath the bark at the collar and this, as mentioned above, is a useful diagnostic feature of the disease (Plate **40**).

In the autumn, characteristic fruit bodies of honey fungus may

84

appear at the base of trees killed by the disease, or on stumps. They are honey-coloured toadstools (Plate **39**) some 7 to 15 cm tall, with caps 5 to 15 cm across. The under-surface of the cap is lined with gills, which usually continue a little way down the stem. The stem near the top has a ragged whitish collar, which appears once the cap has expanded. The toadstools usually appear in clumps in September or October and are destroyed by the first keen frosts.

Several chemicals have been claimed to give control but, in most situations in this country, there is so far no satisfactory alternative to the complete removal or destruction of infected roots and stumps. Observations over a period of years have indicated that a number of tree species appear to be relatively resistant to the disease. For further information on the susceptibility of different tree species, the reader is referred to the list for further reading at the end of this chapter.

Phytophthora root rot

Phytophthora root rot (Plate **41**) is a less well-known, but certainly very important, disease of a wide range of trees, both broadleaved and coniferous. A number of different *Phytophthora* species can cause root rot but their individual characteristics can only be determined by detailed microscopic studies in the laboratory.

The name 'root rot' is somewhat misleading for, although the fungus enters and kills the roots of trees, it does not cause any decay. The above-ground visual symptoms of disease include yellow or small leaves and die-back or death of the tree. These symptoms are, however, found with many root diseases and diagnosis of phytophthora root rot is notoriously difficult. In some instances, a more characteristic symptom may be present at the base of the stem. Dead bark may extend from the roots up the stem for some 10 cm or more, in the shape of a tongue or elongated strip. If the bark is cut away in this region, the infected discoloured bark tissue can be distinguished from the lighter-coloured healthy parts. However, this symptom is not diagnostic of phytophthora root rot, as it can be caused by a number of other agencies, such as lightning or fire.

The *Phytophthora* species causing this disease are microscopic fungi, which do not possess fruit bodies visible to the naked eye. The tiny spores are well-adapted to living in soil, particularly when it is wet. They can swim through wet soil and can be carried through drainage water in order to infect new host trees. Trees infected with phytophthora root rot are therefore often found on sites which are subject to waterlogging. Such waterlogging need not be a permanent feature of the site and water standing for a few hours may be sufficient to allow spores to move and cause a new infection.

The most important means of combating phytophthora root rot is to avoid planting trees on sites known to be subject to waterlogging. It is also, perhaps, worth bearing in mind that this disease is not necessarily fatal and, in some cases, trees can recover. However, it can be a particularly serious problem in nurseries, and chemical treatments are currently being developed to deal with the problem in this situation.

Oak wilt

This is a serious disease of oak in North America and, although not found in this country, it has been the subject of considerable interest in Britain because of the overriding importance of oak in the British town- and land-scape.

Oak wilt is caused by the fungus *Ceratocystis fagacearum*, a relative of the fungus causing Dutch elm disease. Indeed, there are a number of similarities between the two diseases, but there are also important differences.

The symptoms of oak wilt include the wilting and discolouration of the foliage. There are two major groups of oaks, and members of the red oak group which are attacked by the disease often die within a few weeks of infection. On the other hand, in the white oak group (to which the native British oaks belong), symptoms are often restricted to certain branches and only limited die-back occurs. However, recurrence of the disease in subsequent years can lead to the eventual death of the tree.

The fungus is spread from infected to healthy trees by two different methods. The roots of neighbouring oaks in North America are often grafted to one another and the fungus is able to spread from one tree to the next through the connected roots. The disease can also be transmitted by a number of insect species and, also, by other animals. Oak-bark beetles are able to spread the disease in the same manner as elm-bark beetles transmit Dutch elm disease. However, the American oak-bark beetles are very inefficient carriers and this method of dispersal is not very successful. In addition, there are other insects and animals, such as birds and squirrels, which can spread the fungus from fungal mats which develop under the bark of dead or dying trees. These fungal mats consist of fungal material which is attractive to animals. They feed on the fungus and can spread its spores to wounds on neighbouring healthy oaks. A wound is essential for successful infection to occur.

The disease was first discovered in Wisconsin in the United States in the early 1940s and, by 1951, it was known to be present in 18 states in the east and central parts of the country. Spread of the disease has occurred only slowly and erratically, through root transmission or via insect vectors. Its known distribution has changed very little in recent years.

Where the disease is a serious problem, it is controlled by the felling and destruction of diseased trees and by the severance of roots connecting infected to healthy trees, in order to prevent root transmission. Such measures are now taken only in a few parts of the United States.

No evidence of the disease has been found in Britain, despite the fact that imports of oak wood from the United States have continued since the disease was first discovered there, nearly 40 years ago. Oaks in this country sometimes show die-back and symptoms of 'stag-headedness' (ends of branches dead and defoliated), but this is not due to oak wilt. It is a complex disorder which probably arises as a result of adverse environmental conditions, such as drought and attacks by relatively minor pests and diseases.

Britain imports substantial quantities of oak wood from North America, notably for furniture and for the whisky trade for the manufacture of barrels. Stringent conditions, however, are laid down for the import of wood to this country. All bark must be removed before shipment and one of several alternative treatments must be applied to the wood. The removal of the bark ensures that any insect vectors of the disease present in the bark are destroyed before export: the other treatments are designed to kill the fungus which might be present in the sapwood.

Oak wilt provides a good example of a serious tree disease not found in Britain and of the types of measure which are taken to safeguard our native oak populations.

TREE DISORDERS

A very wide range of environmental factors can, from time to time, cause damage to trees, including climatic factors such as frost, drought and lightning, and other factors such as chemical poisoning or unsuitable soil types. It is not possible to discuss all such factors here but two examples have been selected as being amongst the more important. These are damage caused by air pollution and that caused directly by man's activities.

Air pollution
Sulphur dioxide, produced by the burning of coal or oil, and motor vehicle fumes emitted from the exhausts of internal-combustion engines, are well-known air pollutants. If present in sufficient quantities, these, and other toxic gases, can damage the health of humans and also of trees. However, we are fortunate in Britain and widespread damage to trees caused by air pollution has not been reported. Locally, severe symptoms have been reported close to major sources of industrial air pollution and tree populations in large industrial conurbations are, perhaps, amongst those at greatest risk.

Sulphur dioxide is the commonest pollutant, as it is produced by many industrial processes, but another gas, hydrogen fluoride, is also important. The exhaust fumes from motor vehicles are directly toxic to plants to only a limited extent but, in the United States, certain secondary products formed as a result of chemical interaction in sunlight have been found damaging.

Sulphur dioxide
Sulphur dioxide is produced in such industrial processes as the burning of coal, oil or gas, in oil refining, and in the smelting and refining of several metal ores. On broadleaved trees, it causes small yellow or brown patches on those parts of the leaf tissues between the veins. However, trees vary in their susceptibility to sulphur dioxide and some species, especially sycamore and London plane, are able to tolerate this pollutant more than others. This is perhaps one reason why these two species are widely planted in some urban parks and streets.

In recent years, there has been an increased awareness of the dangers of air pollution and industrial companies are taking concerted action to reduce emissions of toxic fumes. In some cases, sulphur dioxide is removed before gaseous products are released into the atmosphere. In others, high chimneys are erected in order to aid dispersion of fumes and to reduce their concentration at ground level. Nevertheless, with ever-increasing industrial output, there seems little doubt that the damaging effects of air pollution will continue for many years.

Hydrogen fluoride
Hydrogen fluoride and another related chemical, silicon tetrafluoride, are important air pollutants. They are produced by a number of chemical processes, including aluminium smelting and the firing of brick and pottery kilns. Fluorides are of special significance, as they can damage plants at very low concentrations. In contrast to sulphur dioxide damage, the symptoms of fluoride damage are concentrated around the margins and at the tips of leaves. There is often a distinct, narrow, reddish-brown line of dead tissue separating healthy from affected parts. A number of species, including London plane, sycamore and lime, tolerate pollution by fluoride gases and this contrasts with the susceptibility shown by many coniferous species.

Vehicle exhaust fumes
In the United States, much research has been undertaken into the effects of vehicle exhaust fumes on vegetation. Studies have been concentrated in large urban areas, such as Los Angeles, where serious pollution dangers have been recognised. During hot, windless, sunny periods, fumes accumulate in such areas and an 'urban smog' may be produced. Various chemical reactions between the products of fuel combustion occur, some requiring the presence of strong sunlight, and a chemical known as PAN is synthesized. This chemical is toxic to plants and causes a glazed or bronzed appearance on the lower surface of the leaves. The climatic conditions needed for this photochemical reaction rarely occur in Britain and damage of this nature is, therefore, likely to be infrequent.

General
Whilst the various symptoms which have been described above are useful indicators of air-pollution damage, such damage can be readily confused with that caused by other agencies. It is also important to recognise that pollution damage may only occur at certain times of the year, when the foliage is particularly susceptible, and that it may be limited to susceptible species. The diagnosis of air-pollution damage must be a task for the experts, in order that proper account is taken of the wide range

of factors which can be operative in a complex urban or industrial environment.

Activities of man

Vandalism is perhaps one of the most serious causes of damage to young trees in some urban areas (Plate **42**). Small, newly-planted trees are broken or uprooted and stakes are removed. The problem may be lessened by the use of fewer, larger plants and firm stakes but it is probably more of a sociological and educational problem than a strictly arboricultural one. The city arborist can, perhaps, play his part by visiting schools and explaining the value of trees in the urban landscape.

The younger generation is not solely responsible for damage to trees: vehicle drivers can be an equal menace. Roadside trees and those situated in car parks are particularly vulnerable to basal damage. Such damage can provide ideal entry points for decay fungi. Care must be taken not to plant trees too close to the kerbside but damage caused by accidents or dangerous driving is difficult to avoid.

Earth-moving activities associated with a number of engineering operations, such as road works, property development or landscaping, can cause serious damage to trees. In many developments, mature trees are retained on the site but their main roots can be readily severed by earth-moving equipment. Great care should be taken to avoid such operations close to these trees.

Changes in soil level can be responsible for death of trees. If additional soil is placed over the original soil surface, any tree roots present will be asphyxiated through lack of oxygen. A similar effect is obtained by covering the soil over the main root system with asphalt or other impervious layers.

Some changes in soil level or surface may be essential for building developments and it is possible, in some circumstances, to accommodate a degree of change without causing severe damage. Trees can withstand limited root pruning and minor changes in soil level, and it may be possible to modify plans so that no major operations are required around trees. The advice of experts should always be sought in such circumstances.

REFERENCES

1 D.A. Burdekin and D.H. Philips, *Some important foreign diseases of*

90

broadleaved trees, Forestry Commission Forest Record 111, London, HMSO, 1977

2 K. St.G. Cartwright and W.P.K. Findlay, *Decay of timber and its prevention,* London, HMSO, 1958

3 J.N. Gibbs, D.A. Burdekin and C.M. Brasier, *Dutch elm disease,* Forestry Commission Forest Record 115, London, HMSO, 1977

4 B.J.W. Grieg and R.G. Strouts, *Honey fungus,* Arboricultural Leaflet No 2, London, HMSO, 1978

5 E.J. Parker, *Beech bark disease,* Forestry Commission Forest Record 96, London, HMSO, 1974

6 T.R. Peace, *Pathology of trees and shrubs,* London, OUP, 1962

7 T.A. Tattar, *Diseases of shade trees,* London, Academic Press, 1978

8 C.W.T. Young, *External signs of decay in trees,* Arboricultural Leaflet No 1, London, HMSO, 1977

5

The impact of the law

David Harte

SECTION 1: LEGAL PROTECTION OF TREES

A. Scope of tree preservation orders

In the modern urban setting, trees are ornaments for the land-scape, providing shade and shelter, reducing pollution, and con-tributing freshness and variety. Their amenity value is legally recognised in s.60 of the Town and Country Planning Act 1971, which empowers a local planning authority to make Tree Pre-servation Orders in respect of individual specimens, groups of

Fig. 5.1.

trees or woodlands, where the authority takes the view 'that it is expedient in the interests of amenity.'[1] Similar protection applies to all mature trees in conservation areas.[2] It is an offence to cut down, uproot or wilfully destroy a protected tree or wilfully to damage, top or lop it in such a manner as to be likely to destroy it.[3] Where a Tree Preservation Order is likely to be broken, a local planning authority may be able to obtain a court injunction forbidding the breach. Breach of an injunction may result in heavier penalties.[4]

By s.60(6), a preservation order does not apply 'to the cutting down, uprooting, topping or lopping of trees which are dying or dead or have become dangerous, or the cutting down, uprooting topping or lopping of any trees in compliance with any obligations imposed by or under an Act of Parliament or so far as may be necessary for the prevention or abatement of a nuisance'.

B. Orders to plant and replant

Under s.59 of the Town and Country Planning Act 1971, in granting planning permission for any development, a local planning authority has a duty to ensure that, whenever it is appropriate, adequate provision is made for the preservation and planting of trees. The opportunity is to be taken to impose Tree Preservation Orders on existing trees but also to make planting new trees a condition of planning consent.

Where a tree, subject to a preservation order, is removed, uprooted or destroyed in contravention of the order or because it is dying, dead or has become dangerous, it must be replaced. [5] If it dies, it should be taken out and replaced. A replacement tree is protected by the original order. The replacement must be at the same place as the original and of an appropriate size and species. The tree owner may apply to the local planning authority to dispense with his obligation to replace his tree.

Trees in conservation areas which enjoy protection must similarly be replaced if they are removed, uprooted or destroyed, or if they die,[6] and here the obligation to replant appears to apply even where the tree is dealt with under statutory powers or to abate a nuisance.[7]

C. Public authority planting powers

1. Powers to plant generally:
In towns, the difficulties of ensuring attractive provision of trees

93

are typical of the problems of managing the townscape generally, so as to create and conserve the best urban environment possible. Powers of local authorities to plant and tend trees may be used to set an example to private landowners and to ensure that there are enough trees in public places. Such powers are particularly appropriate to ensure that roads are integrated into the townscape.

Local authorities may ensure that there is suitable tree-planting on land which they have themselves acquired for development, in public open spaces or parks which they provide, and in the grounds of local-authority buildings, such as offices, schools and fire stations.

2. Planting on highways:

There are various special powers for tree-planting and maintenance in relation to highways (Plate **43**). Under the Highways Act 1980, s.96, power to improve the appearance of highways specifically includes the power to plant, maintain and protect trees. Local authorities, including parish councils, have these powers in respect of roads for which they are not the highway authorities, provided the highway authority consents.

By the Highways Act 1980, s.142, a highway authority may licence occupiers or owners of premises adjacent to a highway to plant and maintain trees there. This may encourage householders to use verges for planting, so as to provide tree screens which are a benefit to themselves and attractive to the public.

It is made clear by s.96(1), that local authorities may maintain and protect trees on highways even when they have not planted these themselves.

The Town and Country Planning Act 1971, ss.212 and 213, enable pedestrian precincts to be made by closing highways to vehicles in the interests of improving amenity, and provide for tree planting in such precincts.

D. Protection of trees by the general law

1. Trespass and nuisance:

As private property, trees are protected by the law of tort. A trespasser who injures a tree may be liable to compensate the owner by paying damages. An industrial concern which harms trees by poisonous fumes may be prevented from emitting further fumes by an injunction [12] from the courts, and may have to pay damages for legal nuisance.

2. Criminal law:

The criminal law protects trees from vandalism. Under the Criminal Damage Act 1971, s.1, it is an offence to destroy or damage property belonging to another without lawful excuse, whether intentionally or by being reckless as to whether any such property would be destroyed or damaged. This applies to trees, except to foliage or fruit where the tree is growing wild, rather than in a garden or some other tended area.

3. Restrictive covenants:

Tree Preservation Orders protect trees even from their owners. A tree owner may also be prevented from damaging his own tree if he, or a previous owner of his land, has entered into a restrictive covenant, an agreement restricting some use of the land for the benefit of neighbouring land.[8] Such a covenant might prevent the cutting down of trees. The law will not normally enforce a positive covenant such as could compel a landowner to maintain trees or replace them if they died. However, under the Housing Act 1974, s.126, local authorities do have powers to enforce covenants, made with them by persons having an interest in land in their areas, to carry out works.

E. Limits to legal protection of trees

1. The need for money and public support:

However wide the legal powers to protect existing trees and plant new ones, the law is of little value without money to provide for policing and planting. Various patterns of land holding may enable local authorities, trusts, or companies operated by residents or others, to look after trees in an area, but the law can only provide a framework. If imaginative use of trees in towns is to be encouraged, public interest and sufficient money are indispensable.

To make Tree Preservation Orders and to keep them up to date is very time-consuming. Even if prosecutions are brought, penalties imposed by the courts for breaking preservation orders or for vandalism are often low and serve as no deterrent. Vandals who damage other people's trees are unlikely to be caught, and the courts do not regard those who desecrate their own property as worthy of particularly severe punishment.

2. Problems in enforcing planting:

The statutory powers requiring replanting of trees are probably the most valuable contribution of the law to conserving urban trees. However, if statutory powers to order planting were fully enforced by local planning officers and arboriculturists, the time needed would be considerable. A major difficulty is that young trees may be planted to comply with an order but die because they are not maintained.

One solution used by certain local planning authorities is to arrange with a developer that its own parks department will do the planting and maintenance, on payment of a suitable fee by the developer. Similarly, local-authority landscape architects may themselves produce schemes for proposed developments, rather than haggle with developers until these come up with something which is just about adequate. However, such arrangements may involve ratepayers in subsidising developers for work which they should have done themselves.

3. The concern of the law with danger and property rights:

Although it does make provision for conservation of trees, the law is more concerned with principles for determining who is responsible for any damage which they may cause.

Trees can pose very real dangers. They may undermine buildings or drop branches on passers-by. Their berries may poison toddlers. If they grow near such a hazard as an electric power line, older children may climb up to it and be electrocuted.

Trees may also conflict with neighbours' enjoyment of their property. The law is a poor machine for assessing aesthetics and, although it may be possible to show that trees generally contribute to the public enjoyment of towns, it may be difficult to weigh up the advantages and disadvantages of particular trees for particular householders. A row of trees, which shelters passers-by and screens one garden, may darken a neighbouring house and block the view of others.

The legal principles which have been developed to deal with damage caused by trees, and with their interference with the property rights of neighbours, may have a tendency to denude towns of trees. It may seem easier to avoid the problems trees can give rise to, simply by not having any.

The remainder of this chapter is, therefore, intended to set out the legal principles of liability for harm caused by trees, identifying who is responsible for particular risks, and suggesting how' prudent recognition of the risks need not be incompatible with extensive use of trees in towns.

SECTION 2: THE TYPES OF LEGAL ACTION TO WHICH TREES MAY GIVE RISE

A. Private nuisance and trespass

There are two forms of legal nuisance, private and public. Private nuisance consists of an indirect interference with someone else's use or enjoyment of their land, or interference with a legal interest in land, such as a right of way. It is an extension of the tort of trespass to land. Trespass involves a direct interference with someone else's possession of land. It would be a direct interference to top a tree so that it fell on a neighbour's garden.

What is direct and what indirect appear to be questions of degree. To cut a tree almost through, so that, an hour later, it fell of its own accord onto a neighbour's garden might well be regarded as trespass. To strip its bark, so that it died and fell a year later, would not, although this could well give rise to liability in nuisance or negligence. What is clear is that allowing a tree to grow on one's own land, or indeed planting it there so that it grows over a boundary, is an indirect, and not a direct, interference with the neighbouring land. Also, felling a tree or allowing it to grow so that it blocks a right of way across the tree-owner's land, will not be a trespass but may be a nuisance.

A characteristic of trespass is that it amounts to a legal wrong, even where it does not result in injury. If a tree is felled onto a neighbouring garden, the garden owner will be entitled to at least nominal damages for trespass even though he has not suffered so much as a dented lawn.

B. Intruding trees – a special form of nuisance

For an action for damages in private nuisance to succeed, injury must be proved. A landowner is generally free to plant any tree he likes on his own land but, as soon as it crosses a boundary, it becomes a peculiar form of legal nuisance, for his neighbour is entitled to cut it back to the boundary, even though it causes no injury to his property, and even though he may cause extreme offence to the tree owner.

1. Cutting without notice:

In *Lemmon* v *Webb*,[9] the House of Lords approved the principle that, if a tree branch projects over neighbouring land, the owner

Fig. 5.2.

of that land may cut it back to the boundary and, provided he does not need to go onto the tree-owner's land, may do so without even giving notice to the tree owner (figure **5.2**). It has been assumed that the same right applies to roots. Lord

Macnaghton in *Lemmon* v *Webb* left open the possibility that, where a tree is small enough for the owner to transplant it if he is given notice, notice should be given before cutting back. However, it is a large tree which will be the greater loss to the amenity of the neighbourhood.

Severed branches or roots, and indeed wind-fall fruit,[10] belong to the tree-owner, and he must be allowed to come and recover them, although they do not have to be actively returned to him. However, this may be little compensation for the loss of shade or a fine view. It is of no comfort to other neighbours and the public, who may lose the benefit of the tree. Although cutting back overhanging branches without warning may be a rare unneighbourly act, the right to do so poses a potential risk that fine specimens in town gardens may be maimed.

If a highway authority owns land on which a road is built, a tree hanging over the road may technically be a private nuisance as against the authority. The authority is unlikely to cut it back unless it is dangerous or an obstruction, in which case the tree will also be a public nuisance. Often, the tree-owner will himself own the soil on which the highway is built and so the tree cannot be a private nuisance.

2. Comparisons of trees with buildings:
In the case of buildings or other artificial projections, it appears that the offended neighbour must give notice, except in an emergency, such as where the building is about to collapse, or where the building-owner was responsible for its erection. In practice, if a building is put up over a boundary, the neighbour will normally object at the time and, rather than physically demolishing it himself, he may prefer a court order, compelling the building-owner to demolish. A tree is in a much more pre-carious position. It may be accepted with pleasure by one neighbour for many years but his successor may dislike it or, one summer, a tree may have grown to a size where a neighbour decides he has had enough of it. If the neighbour does decide he has had enough, he may feel inclined to cut the tree back himself without warning and without going to the expense of employing a competent tree-surgeon. If the tree becomes dangerous to passers-by, the neighbour may be liable in negligence to any who are injured but, if he merely makes the tree unsightly, he is within his rights.

Most significantly, here, if an artificial projection or building erected over a boundary meets with no objection from the neighbour on the other side of the boundary, a right will be acquired by prescription for it to be left. Under the Prescription Act 1832, this will generally arise after 20 years. No such right can be acquired in respect of a tree. However long it has been growing, it is at risk from a neighbour who takes exception to it. As Lindley L.J. explained in *Lemmon* v *Webb*, 'new wood not only lengthens but thickens old wood, and that new wood gradually formed over old wood cannot practically be removed as it grows, and considering the flexibility of branches and their constant motion, it is plain that the analogy sought to be established between an artificial building or projection hanging over a man's land and a branch of a tree is not sufficiently close to serve any useful purpose'.

3. No protection from Tree Preservation Orders:
Even a Tree Preservation Order may not protect a tree which grows across a boundary. Such an order does not prevent any act necessary to abate a nuisance and a tree crossing a boundary is technically a nuisance. If a tree is known to have been planted on one side of the boundary, or if its root system is predominantly on one side, it will belong to the owner of that land, and constitute a nuisance if it encroaches on his neighbour's land.

However, if a trunk actually straddles a boundary and there is no evidence who planted the tree, the adjacent landowners are owners in common. In this case, the tree is not a nuisance[11] and both owners would presumably be bound by a Tree Preservation Order.

C. Damage by intruding trees

1. Cases where there is liability:
If a tree which crosses a boundary causes harm, damages may be recovered for this, and an injunction obtained,[12] requiring the tree-owner to prevent further harm. Normally, a landowner will only be liable for a nuisance originating on his property if he was himself responsible for starting it, or knew, or should reasonably have known, of its existence, and then failed to take reasonable steps to deal with it.

On these principles, the tree-owner should avoid liability if he did not plant the tree himself and had no reason to expect that it had crossed a boundary at all.

The most frequent forms of damage caused by trees are likely to be those underground.[13] A tree-owner clearly cannot tell exactly what his tree roots are doing below ground but it seems that, if his tree is near a boundary, he will certainly be expected to foresee the danger of its roots undermining and so damaging property across the boundary. It appears to make no difference whether the tree was self-sown or planted.[14]

Similarly an owner could hardly claim that there was no reason for him to anticipate damage where a tree physically pushes down a wall on adjacent property, or prises off guttering.

2. Foreseeability of damage in nuisance:

It has been held that, in nuisance generally, there is only liability for damage of a type which was reasonably foreseeable.[15] Exactly what was foreseeable in any particular case is a question of fact. If a tree projects over a boundary (Plate **45**), its owner should doubtless foresee that, if it should happen to fall, it could damage a car parked under it. It is unlikely that he would be expected to have foreseen that it might cause a gas main to explode and blow up the whole neighbouring house. If the tree-owner had no reason to know that his tree branch was likely to fall, a court might now even take the view that any damage caused by the branch, if it did fall, was damage of an unforeseeable type. This would mean that the tree-owner would be unlikely to have to pay damages, even if he caused a nuisance, unless he was negligent.

Certain types of damage may clearly be foreseeable simply as a result of a tree being there. Leaves may clog a neighbour's gutter, and cause damp, perhaps leading to dry rot. Leaves may damage a lawn. Birds nesting in a tree may foul stonework. Trees with particular characteristics may bring their own problems. The lime, with its tendency to attract aphids producing honeydew, may mean that cars left beneath are likely to be smeared.

However, these types of damage are so commonplace and can so often be guarded against by the party affected, that courts would normally be unsympathetic to claims in respect of them.

D. Indirect damage by tree roots

1. Extraction of water:

Apart from causing direct damage to foundations, tree roots may affect the water level in the subsoil and, indirectly, cause subsidence. Particularly if the soil consists of certain types of clay, extraction of water may cause it to contract considerably. If this process takes place as a result of roots which have grown across a boundary, onto land where the subsidence occurs, there will clearly be liability. If the roots do not cross the boundary, however, the tree-owner has a right to the water on his own land, even if extracting it affects his neighbour. This follows from

Fig. 5.3.

Bradford Corporation v *Pickles*,[16] where a landowner actively extracted water on his own land and interfered with its percolating through into the corporation's reservoir, apparently in revenge for the corporation's refusal to buy his land, so as to include it with the reservoir.

2. Heave:
Subsidence may result where a tree is cut down and the soil heaves up, as it recovers the moisture previously extracted by the tree. A building erected where it is affected by a tree whose roots have crossed the boundary from neighbouring land may be at risk if the tree is felled. If the tree is old, it may need to be felled for safety reasons. It is possible that a landowner wishing to build could claim for the cost of additional foundations, which would safeguard against future heave, or for the expense of removing the protruding roots and waiting for the land to correct

102

itself before he built. However, only such cost as was strictly necessary could be recovered and not the cost of exaggerated precautions. Once the building was up, if the tree were felled, there would seem less possibility of recovery of damages for the effects of heave by the owner of the building. The tree-owner would merely be abating a nuisance.

E. A dangerous state of affairs as a nuisance

A state of affairs which is a continuing source of danger may be a nuisance.[17] A tree the roots of which are damaged or which is rotten and so likely to fall across a boundary is likely to constitute a private nuisance even before it actually falls, and an injunction could be obtained by a threatened neighbour to make its owner deal with it. However, a tree which is not in a dangerous state and has not yet extended beyond its owner's boundary can hardly be regarded as a nuisance, even if it is likely to begin causing damage once it does cross the boundary, perhaps by undermining foundations.

If a building has been made unsafe by tree action, it may constitute a private nuisance to neighbouring property. If the dangerous state should be apparent to the owner, he will be liable for damage caused if it does collapse. He may even be liable if the dangerous condition would have been apparent had he inspected it, even though he was not unreasonable in being unaware of it. This could be so if he conducted regular inspections but the damage had appeared since the last one.[18]

F. Shade, light and the view

1. Shade of overhanging trees:
Disputes may arise where a tree restricts light to a neighbouring house or garden (Plate **46**). If the tree overhangs the boundary, the neighbour has his remedy of cutting it back. If it harms his plants, he may be able to recover damages from the courts. In *Smith* v *Giddy*,[19] an owner of ash and elm trees was ordered to pay damages where these overhung neighbouring fruit trees and limited their yield.

2. Interference with light to neighbouring buildings:
Even if a tree does not cross a boundary, its owner may be liable in private nuisance if it affects light next door. What a neighbour may at first regard as a pleasant screen may become a gloomy

barrier. Although tree-owners cannot acquire, by long use, a right to have their trees extend beyond their boundaries, among the rights which may be acquired by long use is a hardly more tangible one, that of light coming from neighbouring land. Such a right over one piece of land for the benefit of another piece of land is an easement and will generally continue, even if both

Fig. 5.4.

pieces of land change hands. If a tree interferes with such a right, a court may award damages and order it to be cut back, even if it does not cross a boundary. Planning permission is unlikely to be given for a building which will severely block light to an existing building but trees may well grow up and interfere with light.

The amount of light for which a person may acquire an easement was stated by Ld. Lindley in *Colls. v Home and Colonial Stores Ltd.*[20] to be 'sufficient light according to the ordinary notions of mankind for the comfortable use and enjoyment of his house as a dwelling house, if it is a dwelling house, or for the beneficial use

Fig. 5.5.

and occupation of the house if it is a warehouse, a shop, or other place of business'.

The Prescription Act 1832 only allows the easement to be acquired for the benefit of 'any dwelling, house, workshop or other building'. It would not be possible to prescribe a right to sunlight to a garden or open place. However, buildings include greenhouses. In *Allen v Greenwood*,[21] the Court of Appeal held that an easement may be acquired for a greenhouse, to sufficient light to enable plants to grow. Generally, a right could be acquired for some special purpose if the purpose was known to the person whose land was to be made subject to the right.

3. Properties of the sun apart from light:
It is difficult to separate light from other properties of the sun, such as heat. Yet if light were not effectively reduced, there would seem to be no cause for complaint if a tree blocked out warmth from a window. In *Allen v Greenwood*, Goff L.J. said he had no doubt that mere interference with warmth in a swimming pool by blocking direct sunlight would not be a nuisance. Both he and Orr L.J. left open the possibility that, where solar heating was installed, a right might be prescribed to warmth.

4. No easement of shelter or a view:
If a tree substantially reduces light to a building, it may, therefore, constitute a private nuisance, even though it does not spread across a boundary. However, no one may acquire an easement to shelter from a tree on neighbouring land, or to the benefits of its attractive appearance or its effect as a screen for something less attractive.[22] As no right has been recognised to the benefits of a fine view, there is no ground for complaint if a tree blocks the view. No right can be acquired to airflow in a particular channel[23] and so no objection could be taken to a tree which made a neighbouring property either stuffy or windy.

Although the rights which may be acquired by way of an easement affecting trees on neighbouring property are limited, restrictive covenants might be created to protect other interests, for example, to prevent the planting of trees so as to block a fine view, or to prevent their being removed unreasonably, where they provide a valuable screen. Such a covenant could be created by a tree-owner and could be attached to his land, so as to continue when the land was disposed of to someone else. However, a restrictive covenant, unlike an easement, could not be acquired simply by long use.

G. Public nuisance

1. The nature of public nuisance:

Unlike private nuisance, public nuisance is essentially a crime. It consists in interfering with the rights of members of the public, or a class of them.[24] Where a tree projects over a public highway, blocking the road or pavement, or where its roots undermine and crack the surface, it may affect any passer-by and, if it amounts to a danger or obstruction, will be a public nuisance.[25] If an individual passer-by suffers some injury peculiar to himself from a public nuisance, he may bring a civil action for damages. In this case, he may also seek an injunction to stop the nuisance. In the absence of such private damage, a member of the public could only bring a criminal prosecution in respect of a public nuisance. Alternatively, the Attorney-General has power to obtain an injunction restraining an interference with a highway. It seems from *Kent C.C.* v *Batchelor*[26] that local authorities may also obtain such injunctions under the Local Government Act 1972, s.222.

2. Trees and buildings as public nuisances:

Where trees invade private property, they are more vulnerable than buildings[27] but, where they extend over a highway (Plate **47**), the law on public nuisance treats them less strictly than buildings. As Rowlatt J. put it, a property owner should not be treated as an 'insurer of nature'.[28]

The Court of Appeal has recognised that there is a strict duty to maintain an artificial structure, such as a lamp, projecting over a highway, whereas the duty to maintain a projecting tree is one of reasonable care.[29] In practice, the distinction may not be very great. The strict liability for an artificial structure only applies if the defect would have been apparent if the owner had looked. Even there, if a trespasser caused the defect, for example, if a vandal had been swinging on an overhanging signboard, the owner would only be liable if he ought reasonably to have noticed the damage.[30] If the damage occurred whilst the owner was away on holiday, he could not have seen it, even if it were obvious.

Although there is no strict duty on occupiers of premises, by highways, to ensure the safety of their trees, there is certainly a duty to take reasonable care. If a tree is defective, in a manner which an ordinary tree-owner would have noticed if he had kept his eyes open, there will be liability for failure to remedy the defect.

Even if the duty to keep buildings by highways safe is greater than the duty to keep trees safe on similar sites, buildings cannot be dispensed with. Trees may be regarded as a luxury and so are still more vulnerable, despite the less onerous duty to maintain them.

H. Negligence

1. The meaning of negligence:
The commonest form of tortious liability for injury of any sort is negligence. As stated by Lord Atkin in what is probably the most famous case in British law, *Donoghue* v *Stevenson*,[31] one must take reasonable care to avoid acts or omissions which one should reasonably foresee would be likely to injure persons who are so closely and directly affected that they ought reasonably to have been contemplated as being so affected. A person who negligently injures another is liable for all damage of a type which he ought reasonably to have foreseen.[32]

2. Negligence compared with trespass and nuisance:
In some circumstances, trespass or nuisance may be established without negligence. A person is responsible for damage caused by a tree which he causes to fall onto neighbouring property or a road by cutting it down, or by damaging its roots in erecting a building beside it, so that it falls some time later. It may not matter if he could not reasonably have foreseen the tree's falling as it did.

However, the tort of negligence extends much further than trespass or private nuisance. These are both wrongs against a neighbour's rights in land. A visitor on that land or even a member of the owner's family, could only sue if he could show negligence. It is probable that the person in possession of the land could sue in private nuisance for physical injury to himself or to his property on the land even where the property is not attached to the land, as in the case of a car.[33]

I. Negligence as a requirement for nuisance

In certain circumstances, negligence is a necessary ingredient in proving nuisance. An occupier of land is only liable for damage resulting from a nuisance he did not create himself, if he realised the nuisance existed, or ought reasonably to have realised, and ought reasonably to have taken steps to deal with it. A person who buys land with a tree with damaged roots may have no reason to know the tree is unsafe. In that case, he will not be liable if it falls and injures someone.

Where a tree projects over a highway and causes an obstruction, it will amount to a public nuisance, but the owner will not be liable unless he ought to have recognised the danger. In *British Road Services v Slater*,[34] a lorry ran into a projecting branch when it pulled over to the side of the road to allow another lorry to pass. A packing case was knocked off and caused the other lorry to crash. It was held that the branch was a nuisance, but the tree owner was not liable, as there was no reason for anyone to have appreciated the danger in advance.

J. Occupiers' Liability Act 1957

The Occupiers' Liability Act 1957 was passed to ensure that occupiers should owe a uniform duty to their various legitimate visitors. Previously, different duties were owed to different classes of visitor. S.2 of the Act imposes a duty to take reasonable care to see that all lawful visitors are reasonably safe in using the premises for the purpose for which they were allowed to enter. Liability might arise where a milkman tripped over a footpath badly cracked by roots or was hit by a falling branch. The Act specifies that the occupier must be prepared for children to be less careful than adults.

This Act does not protect trespassers but it appears that an occupier owes even these a duty to act in accordance with the dictates of common humanity.[35] This would mean that an occupier would probably be liable to a child who fell down from a clearly rotten branch or was electrocuted on a cable passing close to a tree, where the occupier was fully aware that children frequently climbed the tree and he took no steps to warn them of the danger.[36]

K. Defective Premises Act 1972

1. Responsibility of an owner continues after lease or sale:

There used to be a rule that, on letting or sale of land, the tenant or purchaser was deemed to accept the premises in the state in which he acquired them so that any responsibility of the landlord or vendor for the safety of visitors ended.

Now, the Defective Premises Act 1972, s.3, ensures that 'where work of construction, repair, maintenance or demolition or any other work is done in relation to premises', the landlord or vendor will continue to be responsible after the lease or sale 'to persons who might reasonably be expected to be affected by defects in the state of the premises created by the doing of the work'. If an owner negligently constructed a building on land which was still rising after the removal of trees, he would still be liable for damage caused by the unsafe building after he had let or sold the premises.

to buildings,[37] in which case s.3 would not apply to work done to a tree, such as bad lopping, which later caused a damaged branch to fall. However, cases decided prior to the Defective Premises Act may well mean that, quite apart from that Act, the negligent landlord and vendor will be unable to escape liability at common law for any positive negligence.[38] There is no doubt that an owner will be liable for his own negligent act after letting or selling his land, such as where he badly lops a tree at the request of the tenant or new owner so that a damaged branch later falls on a visitor.

2. Special duty of vendors:
S.1 of the Defective Premises Act 1972 imposes a duty on a person taking on work for, or in connection with, the provision of a dwelling, whether this involves a completely new building, or an enlargement or conversion of any existing building. This provision is limited in its effect. It only applies to dwellings and, even then, developments may be excluded if they are covered instead by special approved schemes made under s.2.[39] Where it does apply, the duty is owed to any persons to the order of whom the building is provided and to anyone acquiring any legal or equitable interest in the property. The work must be 'done in workmanlike or, as the case may be, professional manner, with proper materials and so that, as regards that work, the dwelling will be fit for habitation when completed'. This would seem to require a dwelling to be erected with proper regard to the effect on its stability of nearby trees.

L. Building regulations

There are no precise statutory specifications as to where trees may be planted in relation to buildings, or how near buildings may safely be sited to existing trees. However, Building Regulations provide general standards which are relevant here. The current regulations were made by the Secretary of State for the Environment in 1976.[40] Under the Public Health Act 1936, as amended by the Health and Safety at Work Act 1974, machinery is laid down requiring plans for buildings to be deposited with district councils.[41] Such local authorities may be liable in negligence if they allow buildings to be erected which do not comply with building regulations.[42] Further, under the Health and Safety at Work Act 1974, s.71, if a building is erected in breach of the regulations and causes death or personal injury, this may, itself, be the basis for civil action against whoever was responsible for the building, in addition to any action which may be brought against him at common law.

In the 1976 regulations, Part C2 requires that building sites 'be effectively cleared of turf and other vegetable matter' and requires proper drainage. The removal of trees from a site could increase the need for artificial drainage.

Part D provides for secure foundations, with particular reference to the need for sufficient depth 'to safeguard against damage by swelling, shrinking or freezing of the subsoil'. Foundations will be deemed satisfactory if they comply with certain British Standard Codes of Practice. Such codes may establish approved practice as to the relationship of trees and buildings generally.[43]

SECTION 3: RESPONSIBILITY FOR DANGERS FROM TREES

A. Owners and occupiers

The person most likely to be liable for damage caused by a tree is its owner. That is, the owner of the land on which the tree grows. However, the land may be occupied by someone different from the owner, and an occupier may be responsible in place of, or as well as, the owner.

1. Tenants:

A tenant may be liable in nuisance if a tree on premises which he occupies causes damage.[44] He will owe a duty to visitors under

111

the Occupiers' Liability Act 1957 and to visitors next door in negligence.

2. *Landlords:*

A landlord will be liable for a nuisance if he caused it himself, or if it existed at the time of letting, and he knew or ought to have known about it at the time.[45] If a landlord lets a house, which later collapses onto neighbouring property, he will be liable if this was caused by tree roots which had begun seriously to undermine the foundations at the time of letting, in a manner which should have been obvious.

Again, a landlord will be liable for a nuisance he did not cause himself, if he is under a duty by the lease to repair defects on the premises, or even if he has retained a right to do so in his own interest, provided in either case he knew, or ought reasonably to have known, of the defect.[46] Such a landlord would be liable to a neighbour for the fall of a rotten branch, if the tenant had told him about this. The neighbour would probably sue the tenant and the landlord and, if he succeeded against both, would recover damages from the one best able to pay, leaving them to determine how to share the cost, depending on the terms of the lease.

A landlord may be liable in negligence to visitors to premises which he has let with already dangerous trees on them.[47].

B. Non-occupiers causing damage

1. *Trespassers and visitors:*

Any person who causes a nuisance will be personally liable for the damage it causes. One who damages a tree so that it becomes dangerous is likely to be personally liable for the consequences to neighbouring property owners and to the public on any adjacent highway. He may also be liable in negligence if the tree falls. If the person causing such damage is a trespasser, he will probably be unknown. A trespasser who is caught may well not be able to afford to pay damages.

2. *Vendors:*

A vendor who was negligent,[48] or caused a nuisance, should remain liable after selling the land. Thus, if a builder buys land to develop and damages tree roots on the site during construction, so that, after he has let or sold off the completed site, a tree falls onto a house next door, he will be liable to the neighbour who is affected.

3. Contractors and architects:
Damage to trees on building sites is likely to be the responsibility of a contractor or of an architect supervising his work.[49] If a tree is damaged by a contractor, the occupier who employed him may be responsible for any nuisance which he causes,[50] although not for his negligence.[51] In *Salsbury* v *Woodland and Others*,[52] a householder employed a contractor to remove a 25-foot hawthorn tree from his garden. This caused the fall of telephone wires onto a road. A neighbour trying to coil up the wires so as to prevent an accident had to jump out of the way and was injured. The Court of Appeal held that the householder was not liable for the contractor's negligence even though the work was carried out near a highway.

If a contractor causes a nuisance, he and the occupier employing him will both be liable. Depending on their contract, one or the other may recover an indemnity from the other. If a contractor is told to plant a mature tree in a place where it hangs over a boundary and its shade damages a neighbour's plants, the contractor should be able to recover a full indemnity from his employer who gave him wrong instructions as to the position of the boundary. If, in putting up a building, a contractor damages tree roots and makes the tree a hazard, the owner may be liable for a resulting nuisance but he may recover an indemnity from the contractor on whose skill he relied.

Where a building's foundations are affected by a dangerous tree, there may well be liability on a person professionally concerned with the planting of the tree or in the siting of the building, even if he was not directly involved on site. Such liability may arise under a contract but a person may be liable where his bad advice causes harm to someone with whom he has no contract. A landscape architect may be liable in negligence to a person whose house is undermined by a tree which he advised planting on neighbouring property. If the tree undermines a house on the land where the tree was planted, he may be liable to a later owner or to a visitor who is injured.

4. Local authorities:
A local authority may be responsible if its officials allow a building to be erected which has unsafe foundations and does not

comply with building regulations. In *Dutton* v *Bognor Regis U.D.C.*,[53] a local authority was liable to the second occupier of a house which had been negligently approved by its surveyor.

This decision was approved by the House of Lords in *Anns* v *London Borough of Merton*,[54] where it was made clear that local authorities are under a duty 'to give proper consideration to the question of whether they should inspect or not', and if they do inspect must take reasonable care 'to secure that the builder does not cover-in foundations which do not comply with byelaw requirements'.[55]

District councils have powers to deal with dangerous trees on private land in their areas. The tree-owner may be charged with the cost if he fails to act himself.[56] District councils and the highway authorities for any road have further special powers to deal with trees which are an obstruction or likely to cause danger on a road or footpath.[57] If a council refuses to consider exercising such powers or exercises them negligently, as by felling a tree so that it causes an accident, it is likely to be liable in negligence.

The responsibility of local authorities may be of particular significance as to the extent to which existing trees are retained near new developments. To avoid any possibility of liability, local authorities may apply pressure to get rid of trees or insist on prohibitively expensive foundations, if existing trees are to be kept.

SECTION 4: THE PRACTICAL IMPLICATIONS OF THE LAW'S CONSTRAINTS

A. The standard of care expected

To avoid being liable in negligence or for allowing a nuisance to continue, a person must exercise reasonable care. What amounts to reasonable care is a question of fact. It is therefore difficult to assess in advance, and those who might be liable for damage from trees may be inclined to keep on the safe side by avoiding having any trees. However, the dangers can be exaggerated.

1. Experts and laymen:

The layman is only expected to act like a reasonable layman. Provided he keeps his eyes open, he will not be liable for dangers resulting from his trees, which would only have been apparent to an expert. In *Caminer* v *Northern and London Investment Trust*,[58] the House of Lords did not hold the owners of an elm liable for the falling of one of its branches on a passing car. Here, the tree-owner was a landlord of a block of flats. Lord Normand indicated that the test of what was reasonable for landlords of commercial property, 'postulates some degree of knowledge on the part of the landlords which must necessarily fall short of the knowledge possessed by scientific arboriculturists but which surely must be greater than the knowledge possessed by the ordinary urban observer of trees or even of the countryman not practically concerned with their care'.[59]

The expert architect or landscape architect who wishes to plant a tree on an urban site, or is concerned about the effect of existing trees, particularly on buildings, must take care in exercising professional judgment but, if he is confident in his judgment, he should not need to take precautions which are out of all proportion to any risk.

2. The nature of the risk and the benefit:
In assessing what is reasonable, the Courts take account of whether a risk is only very slight and whether any damage resulting from the risk is likely to be slight.[60] A slight risk, with a slight prospect of damage, may not be unreasonable. In *Caminer's* case, Lord Ratcliffe indicated that there may be a 'difference between the legal responsibilities adjacent to a busy street, and the responsibilities of the owner of a stand of timber bordering a country lane'.[58] Thus, more care may be expected in a town to ensure that mature trees do not become a hazard, because, if a branch falls, it is more likely to hit someone.

On the other hand, where there is a duty of care in siting trees in relation to buildings, or buildings in relation to trees, a remote possibility of slight cosmetic damage from cracks may not be sufficient to require enormous and costly foundations, or the omission of all trees from a planting scheme.

If a risk is taken for reasons of overriding importance, this may make the risk reasonable.[61] In *Quinn v Scott*,[62] the National Trust was held liable for the fall of a tree even though the court recognised the amenity value of trees on Trust property, as human safety was a superior good. However, it may be that, where tree roots are not likely to endanger human safety, the amenity value of having trees in an area would be regarded by a court as outweighing some risk of cosmetic damage, and such inconvenience from slight subsidence as sticking doors or windows.

3. Excessive burden on the defendant:

In circumstances where a nuisance arises through no fault of the owner of a tree, he has a duty to take reasonable steps to remedy it. What is reasonable depends upon his capacity. In *Goldman v Hargrave*,[63] an Australian case, a red gum tree was struck by lightning. The farmer who owned the tree took inadequate precautions to put out the fire and was held liable when it spread. However, Lord Wilberforce, delivering the opinion of the Privy Council, stressed that account must be taken of the ability of the defendant to cope with the situation. 'The standard ought to be to require of the occupier what is reasonable to expect of him in his individual circumstances. Thus, less must be expected of the infirm than of the able-bodied: the owner of a small property where a hazard arises which threatens a neighbour with substantial interests should not have to do so much as one with larger interests of his own at stake and greater resources to protect them: if the small owner does what he can and promptly calls on his neighbour to provide additional resources, he may be held to have done his duty: he should not be liable unless it is clearly proved that he could, and reasonably in his individual circumstances should, have done more.'

If a tree is rendered unsafe by a trespasser or by lightning, the really impecunious householder may have some sympathy from the law if he cannot immediately remedy the defect himself. However, if he has, himself, made the tree dangerous, he will be allowed no leeway.

B. Approved practice

1. Approved practice and professional judgment:

Generally, a court will regard compliance with approved practice as sufficient indication that reasonable care has been shown.[64] However, there is no negligence in failing to follow the normal practice, if that is unduly strict.[65] On the other hand, compliance with approved practice is no excuse in circumstances where, clearly, more care should have been taken.[66] It is generally recognised that poplars and willows are trees the roots of which may give rise to particular problems. Therefore, they are not usually to be planted near buildings. However, it would not be negligent for a landscape architect to include a willow in a planting scheme, if he were confident from his expert knowledge that, on the particular site, it would not cause problems.

On the other hand, planting some rare species with exceptionally powerful roots, which was not a poplar or willow, at the distance where a sycamore might be safe, would not be acceptable simply because the normal practice was only to give extra protection with poplars and willows. Professional judgement must still be exercised in each case.

2. British standards and other Codes of Practice:

Advice published by public bodies on the relationship of trees to buildings, provides examples of approved practice. Its legal authority is limited, but fears have been expressed that certain codes may be used as absolute rules banning trees from anywhere remotely near a building. Insurance companies could use them to justify denying insurance cover and building societies as a basis for refusing mortgages.

In 1978, reports appeared of a proposed British Standards Code of Practice from the British Standards Institute.[67] After fierce reaction from landscape architects to the original draft, the code appeared in 1980 as B.S. 5837: 1980, and is primarily aimed at encouraging responsible and imaginative use of trees in relation to buildings. It counsels protection of existing trees by taking precautions in construction work by minimising the stripping of top soil and by excluding harmful substances like oil, tar and bitumen, and harmful processes like cement mixing or work with cranes. Suggestions are given for avoiding the need to remove trees, such as bridging roots, pruning branches and rerouting underground services. However, B.S. 5837 refers to the earlier code of Practice 2004 of 1972 on Foundations under 1m at a distance from any tree of at least that tree's mature height. The 1979 Handbook of the National Housebuilding Council in practice note 3 warns that on any soil it is unwise to build nearer to a tree than 4.0 m or one-third of its mature height, whichever is less.

However, C.P. 2004 recognises that in the last resort what counts is professional judgment, by recommending that in cases of doubt specialist advice should be sought. B.S. 5837 stresses the need for co-operation between developers, their professional teams and local planning authorities. Because of the variation between soils it stresses that acknowledged local experience provides the best guide for safe planting distances from buildings.

117

C. Professional expertise

1. Choice of site, materials and design:

In constructing buildings, architects and others with specialised skills will be liable if they create a nuisance, for example, by damaging a tree, even if they could not have foreseen danger. They may well be liable under contract to the site-owner to indemnify him if he has to pay damages for the nuisance. Professional indemnity insurance is essential for covering such liability. To rule out any possibility of such liability could reduce the art of the architect solely to the skill of a building safety officer.

In practice, if an architect or landscape architect designs a scheme in a manner which he is confident will satisfy his client, he should avoid such risks as would be likely to make him liable in negligence. Familiarity with soil qualities and the presence of services above ground, like cables, or below ground, like mains and drains, will be necessary in building, even in the absence of trees. If there are trees, or if trees are intended as part of a development, the architect may be expected to know the likely effects of such trees himself or at least to obtain advice from a specialist who does.

In his professional judgement, the architect needs to assess whether it would be unreasonable not to encase drain joints in concrete or provide flexible joints, so as to avoid damage from tree roots. He needs to assess the depth of foundations which is reasonably necessary to safeguard against subsidence caused by tree roots. He may need to assess the time to leave before building after removing a large tree, so that the ground will heave back to its proper state.

2. Knowledge of species:

An architect without specialist knowledge of trees will be wise to call in someone, such as a landscape architect or an arboriculturist, with such knowledge, where the characteristics of particular species are important. More may be expected of the architect than of the ordinary householder who allows self-seeded trees to continue growing in his garden or even buys trees from a nursery to plant at home.

Selection of a species which does badly in towns because of inability to deal with pollution could give rise to liability to the client for the cost of replacement with something more suitable.

118

Choice of trees with unusual root spread or which are well known to extract exceptional quantities of water from the soil may well give rise to liability for resulting subsidence.

Although certain trees are known to cause more problems than others, the courts are a long way from ruling common species out of bounds in towns altogether. Thus in *Caminer* v *Northern and London Investment Trust*[68], Lord Porter quoted an expert witness who had described the elm as 'rather a maligned tree'. 'I know that elms have a higher percentage of heart rot for the species than other trees, but there are an awful lot of elms in the country which have not.' However, the prevalence of Dutch elm disease may mean that elm planting in towns is now unlikely.

Poisonous trees may pose a risk on certain sites. Here, what is reasonable might depend on whether a tree were planted or left in a primary school ground, or in the garden of an old people's home. Cases on poisonous trees are largely concerned with cattle eating yew leaves. There, liability has only been recognised where trees had extended over a boundary[69] or where a tree-owner was under a duty to fence his property.[70] However, in a town, poisonous berries are likely to attract children.[71] Even if they trespass to eat these, the owner may well be liable, and an architect designing a scheme with such a tree in an obviously unsafe place could well be directly liable in negligence to children who were injured.

SECTION 5: LIMITS ON LIABILITY

Those who are fearful of being liable for risks from trees, especially in causing subsidence, may find some reassurance in principles of the law aimed at reducing liability.

A. Contributory negligence

Under the Law Reform (Contributory Negligence) Act 1945, if a person seeking damages for the negligence, or indeed, trespass or nuisance, of another, has partly brought about his own loss by a failure to take reasonable care in his own interest, this is a defence and the court may make an appropriate reduction from any damages it awards.

Thus, if a tree is undermining a building, and the occupier knows this and does nothing about it, his damages could well be

119

reduced because of his failure to mitigate his own loss. In such circumstances, it may not be feasible for him to do expensive remedial work himself but, if he is to recover maximum damages from his neighbour or his architect who allowed the tree to stand so near the building, or from the local authority whose building inspector passed the foundations, he should be able to show that he gave them an early chance to put matters right and keep cost to a minimum.

B. Long-term damage

A concern of the law is to prevent actions arising too long after the incidents on which they are based. The Limitation Act 1980 debars actions brought more than six years from when the cause of action accrued. Where the claim is for damages for personal injury the time is three years.[72]

1. From when does time run?

Where a branch or tree falls, the time for a claim will run from the date of the accident, and any person liable will be in a fairly clear position. He is likely to have recently been at fault in failing to check the tree. However, where a tree gradually undermines foundations, the liability of the person originally responsible for bad siting or construction may not be apparent for a long time. It may be years before damage occurs. This may put the oringinal architect or builder in a difficult position. Nevertheless, in *Sparham-Souter* v *Town and Country Developments (Essex) Ltd.,*[73] the Court of Appeal ruled, in the words of Lord Denning M.R., 'When building work is badly done – and covered up – the cause of action does not accrue, and the time does not begin to run, until such time as the plaintiff discovers that it has done damage, or ought with reasonable diligence, to have discovered it'. There, a local authority was being sued for negligence in not preventing houses from being constructed on poor foundations.[74]

Lord Denning commented in conclusion that 'the only owner who has a cause of action is the owner in whose time the damage appears'. From this it would seem that, if cracks appear in a building as a result of foundations which were inadequate, because of neighbouring trees, an action would need to be brought by the person who was the occupier of the building at the time the cracks appeared.

However, in *Masters* v *Brent London Borough Council,*[75] a father transferred his leasehold interest in a house to his son so that the

Plate 29. Stump removal: a Vermeer stump grinder removing a 6ft diameter stump (see p. 65). Photo: Peter Bridgeman

Plate 30. Brushwood chipper: the Woodchuck Brushwood Chipper reducing volume of brushwood (see p. 65). Photo: Peter Bridgeman

Plate 31.   Anthracnose of London plane (see p. 72).

Plate 31.   Anthracnose of London plane (see p. 72).

Plate 32.   Bacterial canker of poplar

Plate 33.   Anthracnose of weeping willow

Plate 34. Fireblight attacking Sorbis aria *(see p. 75)*

*Plate 35. Dutch elm disease killing Wheatley elm (*Ulmus carpinifolia var sarniesis*). (see p. 76)*

Plate 36. Dutch elm disease: galleries of Scolytus scolytus *in elm bark* (*see p.* 77)

Plate 37. Uprooted beech with severely decayed roots (*see p. 81*)

Plate 38.   Beech bark disease: tarry spots on beech trunk (see p. 79)

Plate 39. Honey fungus: toadstools of **Armillaria** mellea (*see p. 84*)

Plate 40. Honey fungus: *white mycelium under bark of injected tree (see p. 84)*

Plate 41. Phyto-phthora *root rot bark at base of trunk cut away to expose tongues of infected tissue (see p. 85)*

Plate 42. Damage by man: effect of vandalism on young trees (see p. 90) (Plates 31–42: Forestry Commission)

Plate 43. Planting on highways: trees set well away from buildings can be allowed more space for growth (see p. 94). Photo: Kathy Stansfield

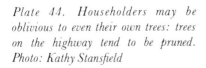

Plate 46 (opposite). A copper beech blocking light to a neighbouring house, even though pruned (see p. 103). Photo: Kathy Stansfield

Plate 44. Householders may be oblivious to even their own trees: trees on the highway tend to be pruned. Photo: Kathy Stansfield

Plate 45. Problems of neighbour's overhanging trees, shade in summer, leaves in autumn (see p. 101). Photo: Kathy Stansfield

Plate 47.   An inoffensive obtrusion onto the highway? Photo: Kathy Stansfield

Plate 48. Savagely pruned tree on pavement: would a reasonable layman think this was safe? Photo: Kathy Stansfield

Plate 49. Interior landscape of new town with mature trees: Cumbernauld New Town Scotland (see p. 132). Photo: The Architectural Press

Plate 50.   Existing trees incorporated into New Town landscape: Peterlee, County Durham (see p. 132). Photo: Architectural Review. Photographer: Eric de Mare

Plate 51.   Landscaped housing for local authority: Coleman's Farm, Surrey (see p. 135). Landscape architects: Brian Clouston and Partners

Plate 52.   Housing landscape at New Ash Green, Kent. Photo: The Architectural Press. Photographer: Selwyn Goldsmith

Plate 53.   Landscaped housing for local authority: Maen Du, Wales (see p. 135). Landscape architects: Brian Clouston and Partners

Plate 54.   Glasgow courtyard at Keppoch: before landscaping

Plate 55. Glasgow courtyard at Keppoch: after landscaping. Landscape architects: Brian Clouston and Partners

son could obtain a mortgage to pay the cost of repairs. The repairs were a result of subsidence caused by the roots of a lime tree for which the Borough Council were responsible.

Talbot J. awarded damages to the son in nuisance, holding that 'Where there is a continuing nuisance inflicting damage upon premises, those who are in possession of the interest may recover losses which they have borne whether the loss began before the acquisition of the interest or whether it began after the acquisition of the interest. The test is: what is the loss which the owner of the land has to meet in respect of the continuing nuisance affecting his land?'.

2. Time is irrelevant where there is no fault:

Case law appears to have created open-ended liability for those responsible for trees which cause damage to foundations. However, a major reservation here is that there will be no liability if there is no fault. An architect who includes trees in a planting design should not be liable in negligence if the trees are planted clearly on his client's land, even if, in twenty or thirty years, they may extend over a boundary.[76] He may properly have expected his client to have them pruned. In these circumstances,he could hardly be said to have caused a nuisance.

One of the main concerns at the reported contents of the 1978 draft standard code of practice, in respect of the siting of buildings in relation to trees, was that it would have imposed restrictions based on the height a tree would attain at maturity, probably not for many years. If architects and landscape architects are careful to explain to clients the need to restrict the height of trees by judicious lopping, and stress that groups of trees may eventually need to be thinned down to single specimens so as to reduce water loss, they may well avoid any implication of negligence if their advice is not followed and foundations are later damaged.

Long-term dangers from trees need to be recognised but, if householders were made more aware of the precautions which could be taken, as much as of the dangers if those precautions are not taken, the fear of any legal liability could be reduced. It would be ironic if existing trees were cut down to avoid liability and this caused much subsidence from land heaving up, especially if this amounted to abating a nuisance and there was no redress at all for the resulting damage.

121

C. Practical limits

The legal effect of tree roots, in particular, raises much uncertainty. The law itself is not entirely clear and, generally, evidence as to the exact effects of roots is difficult to establish. A party claiming damages must prove that the damage resulted from the intruding roots. It may appear that subsidence would have resulted anyway, perhaps because of the naturally shrinkable nature of the soil, or because of effects on the water table which had nothing to do with the intruding tree. The building-owner's own trees or other neighbouring trees may have been involved. The tree-owner may escape liability altogether or only have to pay part of the costs of repair.

Fear of legal liability for various forms of damage by trees could threaten the existence of trees in towns. However, the uncertainty of the law may be offset, by those who could be liable, with sensible insurance arrangements. The possibility of danger from trees cannot be avoided altogether, any more than can the other risks of everyday living. Those who appreciate the value which trees make to the quality of life in towns have the task of persuading others that that value outweighs such risk as cannot be avoided.

REFERENCES

1 Since the Local Government, Planning and Land Act 1980, s.90 and sched. 15, orders will generally be made by district councils. 'Trees' are not defined in the Act but botanical definitions emphasise the characteristics of a perennial plant with a self-supporting main stem or trunk growing to a considerable size. A shrub is a more modest plant, which would not be covered by a tree preservation order. However, young or small trees may be subject to protection. S.59 of the 1971 Town and Country Planning Act enables a local authority to require tree-planting as a condition for permitting development of a site. S.60(3) makes it clear that a preservation order may apply 'from the time when those trees are planted'. 'Amenity' is not defined but, in a different context, has been said to refer to 'pleasant circumstances, features or advantages'; *per* Scrutton L.J. in *Re Ellis and Ruislip U.D.C.* [1920] 1 K.B. 343.

2 S.61A, added by the Town and Country Amenities Act 1974, s.8. More detailed regulations are provided in statutory instruments, S.I. 1969 No. 17 and S.I. 1975 No. 148. Owners and occupiers of land to be affected by a tree preservation order must be notified. If they object, the order will not become effective until it has been confirmed. Since the Local Government, Planning and Land Act 1980, confirmation is by the local planning authority which must hold a public inquiry if there are objections to the order. Because of the requirement of confirmation there would be a danger of tree-owners removing trees as soon as they were notified of an order. To avoid this, s.61 of the 1976 Act provides for provisional tree preservation orders which are effective immediately, for six months.

3 Town and Country Planning Act 1971, s.102.

4 *Kent County Council* v *Batchelor* [1978] 3 All E.R. 980. Talbot J.

5 Town and Country Planning Act 1971, s.62.

6 *ibid* s.61A(8)

7 Machinery for enforcing replanting generally is provided in s.103. The local planning authority may give precise directions as to replanting, if the tree owner fails to do this himself, up to four years from when his duty arises. As a last resort, under s.91, the authority may plant a replacement tree or trees itself and charge the cost to the landowner.

8 *Tulk* v *Moxhay* (1848) 2 Ph. 774.

9 [1895] A.C. 1, affirming the Court of Appeal at [1894] 3 Ch. 1.

10 *Mills* v *Brooker* [1919] 1 K.B. 555.

11 *Holder* v *Coates* (1827) Moody and Malkin 112, *cf. Waterman* v *Soper* (1968) 1 Ld. Raymond 737. Kay L.J. discusses this matter in *Lemmon* v *Webb*, *supra*, note 9, Court of Appeal at page 20. In *Richardson* v *Jay* (1960) E.G. 9 July, the parties were held to own a tree in common. One of them was permitted to cut roots on his own side but was not to fell the whole tree without the consent of his neighbour.

12 High Court powers to grant injunctions are provided for in the Supreme Court of Judicature Act 1925, ss. 18 and 45, and the Rules of the Supreme Court 1965, Order 29, rule 1. County Court powers are provided in the County Courts Act 1959, s.74 and the County Court Rules 1936, Order 13, rule 8.

13 *Morgan* v *Khyatt* [1964] 1 W.L.R. 475, P.C. from New Zealand; *Butler* v *Standard Telephones and Cables Ltd.* [1940] 1 K.B. 399 or [1940] 1 All E.R. 121; *McCombe* v *Read* [1955] 2 Q.B. 429 or [1955] 2 All E.R. 458.

14 *Davey* v *Harrow Corporation* [1958] 1 Q.B. 60 or [1957] 2 All E.R. 305, at p. 71 or 309f *per* Lord Goddard.

15 *The Wagon Mound (No. 2)* [1967] 1 A.C. 617, or [1966] 2 All E.R. 709; Privy Council from Australia, *per* Ld., Reed at p. 640 or 717.

16 [1895] A.C. 587.

17 *Spicer* v *Smee* [1946] 1 All E.R. 489.
18 See here *Wringe* v *Cohen* in public nuisance, *post*, note 29.
19 [1904] 2 K.B. 448.
20 [1904] A.C. 179 at p. 208.
21 [1979] 1 All E.R. 819.
22 *Phipps* v *Pears* [1965] 1 Q.B. 76.
23 *Bryant* v *Lefever* (1879) 4 C.P.D. 172.
24 *Attorney/General* v *PYA Quarries Ltd.* [1957] 2 Q.B. 169 or [1957] 1 All E.R. 894.
25 Allowing trees to grow across a highway probably does not amount to the statutory offence of wilfully obstructing a highway under the Highways Act 1980, s.137. *Walker* v *Horner* (1875) 1 Q.B.D. 4 and *Gully* v *Smith* (1883) 12 Q.B.D. 121.
26 *Supra,* note 4.
27 *Supra,* p.99.
28 *Noble* v *Harrison* [1926] 2 K.B. 332.
29 *Wringe* v *Cohen* [1940] 1 K.B. 229, comparing *Tarry* v *Ashton* (1876) 1 Q.B.D. 314 and *Noble* v *Harrison, supra,* note 28.
30 *Tarry* v *Ashton, supra,* note 29, *per* Blackburn J.
31 [1932] A.C. 562.
32 *The Wagon Mound* [1961] A.C. 338, or [1961] 1 All E.R. 404; Privy Council from Australia.
33 F.H. Newark in 'The boundaries of nuisance' (1948) 65 *Law Quarterly Review* 480, has argued that, in private nuisance, there should only be liability for injury to the interest in the land itself, e.g. for undermining a building.
34 [1964] 1 W.L.R. 498 or [1964] 1 All E.R. 816.
35 *British Railways Board* v *Herrington* [1972] A.C. 877 or [1972] 1 All E.R. 749, House of Lords.
36 The owner of an electrical power line on land which he does not himself own may be liable in negligence to persons electrocuted on it, irrespective of whether the person injured was a trespasser. *Buckland* v *Guildford Gas Light and Coke Co.* [1949] 1 K.B. 410.
37 In *Metropolitan Water Board* v *Paine* [1907] 1 K.B. 285, the term 'premises' in one statute was limited to buildings. In *Whitley* v *Stumbles* [1930] A.C. 544, it was given a broader meaning in relation to another statute.
38 *Dutton* v *Bognor Regis U.D.C.* [1972] 1 Q.B. 373 or [1972] 1 All E.R. 462, Court of Appeal, Ld. Denning M.R. at p. 394 or 472. Approved by the House of Lords in *Anns* v *London Borough of Merton* [1978] A.C. 728 or [1977] 2 All E.R. 492.
39 These include the 10-year protection scheme of the National House-Builders' Registration Council, which provides a guarantee similar to the cover of s.I., House Building Standards (Approved Scheme etc) Order 1979, S.I. 1979 No. 381.
40 S.I. 1976 No. 1676. Previous regulations apply to buildings cons-

tructed before or in accordance with plans deposited before 31st January 1977. Building regulations are made under the Public Health Act 1936, ss.61 and 62 as substituted by the Health and Safety at Work Act 1974, s.61.

41 Health and Safety at Work Act 1974, s.76(2). In London, the provisions apply to the Greater London Council and London borough councils.

42 See *post* p.113.

43 See *post* p.117.

44 *Wilchick* v *Marks and Silverstone* [1934] 2 K.B. 56.

45 *Brew Bros. Ltd.* v *Snax (Ross) Ltd.* [1970] 1 Q.B. 612 or [1970] 1 All E.R. 587. *cf St. Anne's Well Brewery Co.* v *Roberts* (1928) 140 L.T.I.

46 *Wilchick* v *Marks and Silverstone, supra,* note 44; *Mint* v *Good* [1951] 1 K.B. 517 or [1950] 2 All E.R. 1159.

47 A landlord owes a wide duty under the Defective Premises Act 1972, s.4, to all persons who might reasonably be expected to be affected by defects in the state of the premises. This is 'to take such care as is reasonable in all the circumstances to see that they are reasonably safe from personal injury or from damage to their property caused by a relevant defect'. This duty only arises, however, where the landlord has an obligation for maintenance under the lease and has learnt, or ought in all the circumstances to have known, of the defect. Provided 'premises' applies to land and not just buildings on land, this should render a landlord liable for failing to remedy a tree which had recognisably become unsafe. See *supra,* p. 110 and the Defective Premises Act 1972, s.3.

48 For liability in negligence, see *supra,* p. 110 and the Defective Premises Act 1972, s.3.

49 S.1 of the Defective Premises Act 1972, should apply to architects and contractors involved in providing dwellings, *supra,* p. 110. A person reasonably relying on the instructions of another has a defence. Thus, if a contractor is sued for subsidence of a building he erected, he might escape liability by showing that the subsidence resulted from heave after removal of trees on the site before he began work, and that he was assured by the architect that this would cause no problems.

50 *Per* Scrutton L.J. in *Job Edwards Ltd.* v *Birmingham Navigations* [1924] 1 K.B. 341 at 355.

51 The occupier will be vicariously liable in negligence if his own employee causes the damage, such as where a caretaker or gardener employed in an office block negligently damages a tree.

52 [1970] 1 Q.B. 324 or [1969] 3 All E.R. 863 C.A.

53 *Supra,* note 38.

54 *Supra,* note 38.

55 The duties under the Defective Premises Act 1972, s.1, probably do

not apply to local authorities concerned with checking foundations. This section imposes a duty of care on those who are 'taking on work for or in connection with the provision of a dwelling'. Unless they are providing council houses, a local authority may not be 'taking on work'. However, a further common law duty may attach to local authorities where they make tree preservations orders, or refuse to grant permission to cut down any tree subject to such an order. If such a tree is dangerous, the local planning authority may be liable to any person who is later injured by it.

56 Local Government (Miscellaneous Provisions) Act 1976, s.23.
57 Highways Act 1980, s.154, and see s.141. S.79 allows for orders altering or restricting planting so as to prevent danger from obscured vision at bends and junctions. Where a tree falls into a highway, there may be a duty on a highway authority to remove it under s.150 of the 1980 Act. Statutory bodies, such as electricity boards and the Post Office, whose work may be hampered by trees, may require tree-owners to lop such trees or, if necessary, do the work themselves. Electricity Supply Act 1926, s.34 and Telegraph (Construction) Act 1908, s.5.
58 [1951] A.C. 88 or [1950] 2 All E.R. 486.
59 At 100 or 493E.
60 *Bolton* v *Stone* [1951] A.C. 850 or [1951] 1 All E.R. 1078.
61 *Watt* v *Herts C.C.* [1954] 1 W.L.R. 835 or [1954] 2 All E.R. 368.
62 [1965] 1 W.L.R. 1004 or [1965] 2 All E.R. 588.
63 [1967] 1 A.C. 645 or [1966] 2 All E.R. 989, Privy Council, from Australia.
64 *Wright* v *Cheshire C.C.* [1952] 2 All E.R. 789.
65 *Brown* v *Rolls Royce Ltd.* [1960] 1 W.L.R. 210 or [1960] 1 All E.R. 577.
66 *Global Dress Co.* v *W.H. Boase & Co.* [1966] 2 Lloyds Rep. 72.
67 Tarsem, Flora, Treeless towns, *Landscape Design*, February 1978, P. 10.
68 *Supra*, note 58.
69 *Crowhurst* v *Amersham Burial Board* (1878) 4 Ex. D.5.
70 *Ponting* v *Noakes* [1894] 2 Q.B. 281.
71 *Glasgow Corporation* v *Taylor* [1922] 1 A.C. 44.
72 Limitation Act.
73 [1976] 1 Q..B 858 or [1976] 2 All E.R. 65. This principle was approved by the House of Lords in *Anns* v *Merton London Borough Council, supra,* note 38.
74 In negligence and nuisance, time usually runs from when damage occurs.An arboriculturist who negligently passed a branch as safe, when it was not, could be sued for personal injuries within three years of when the branch fell and hit someone, even though it did not fall till some time after the inspection. A claim under the Defec-

tive Premises Act 1972, s.1. runs from when building has been completed. If remedial work is done and this also is defective, time for any action in respect of the further work runs from when it was completed.

75 [1978] 1 Q.B. 841 or [1978] 2 All E.R. 664.

76 He might be liable to his client, in contract, or even to his client's successor, in negligence, if he recommended trees which soon grew too large but which he, mistakenly, thought were dwarf species.

6

Managing the landscape of towns

Chris Wild

Recognition of the need for landscape management plans for our towns is an expression of the increasing importance placed upon the value of green spaces in the urban environment. Chapter 1 outlined the place of trees in the urban environment from a historical and design viewpoint. Subsequent chapters concentrated largely on the practical advantages and problems associated with trees as the landscape element which has the greatest impact on our towns. This chapter broadens the discussion to include the need for, and maintenance of, green spaces, the covering of areas with street trees, urban parks, and revegetated urban wastelands, and looks at the different ways in which amenity and open space have been regarded in our towns.

GREEN SPACES IN TOWNS

The earliest towns had their areas of communal green space – the 'moor' in the north of England, and the 'common' in the south – upon which the town dweller had the right to graze cattle. They were relics of a pre-industrial society where the household economy consisted of part-time work at a trade and part-time management of a small holding. The green space was not an amenity: it was productive land, a central element in the town's economy. Such spaces tended to be lost as towns spread and became industrialised. Where the town had grown from a village the agriculture of which was based on the 'three-field' system, its development was often strongly affected by the attitudes of townspeople to this communal land.

    W.G. Hoskins in *The Making of the English Landscape'* [1] describes how the development of three closely-related towns Nottingham, Leicester and Stamford was constrained by traditional agriculture. Under the 'three-field' system, the burgesses of the town had Lammas pasture rights which allowed them to graze cattle over the common fields after the harvest. This right was used to prevent the growing Victorian towns from spreading outside the eighteenth-century boundaries, and enclosing the open fields and using them for housing land. Nottingham failed to solve the problem until 1845, when the population of the town was crammed into a dense area of slum housing. Leicester, a market town similar to Nottingham in the eighteenth century, managed to use the former open fields for housing before the need became too great, and the town grew and incorporated 'large gardens, even in the centre of town', 'wide streets', 'ample yards' and, often, little gardens. The burgesses of Stamford, a town which was similar in the eighteenth century to Nottingham and Leicester, opposed any building on the open fields for political reasons. This effectively blocked any growth of the town. Because of lack of land, the London-to-York railway was routed through Peterborough, instead of Stamford as was originally proposed, and the town ossified in its eighteenth-century form. Essentially, however, the present-day existence of urban commons and of remnants of the open fields, which may have been incorporated into the fabric of the town, is adventitious and unplanned.

During the eighteenth century, the earlier examples of Georgian town houses were built by speculative developers. The houses were designed by architects and, frequently, planned in squares or terraces fronting on to open space. Originally, the square was paved and intended for the parking of carriages, but it was later fenced and planted with trees and shrubs. It was an amenity available to the relatively wealthy residents of the houses, who shared maintenance costs and each possessed a key which gave entry to the square. The Georgian squares were a private amenity for the benefit of house-owners but which made a contribution to the environment of the whole town. This tradition continues today, and it is the residents of the squares of Cheltenham and the new town in Edinburgh who are responsible for the upkeep of the gardens and who enjoy the private rights of access.

VICTORIAN ATTITUDES TO OPEN SPACE

On the basis of wealth derived from industries, the coalfields and the colonies, industrial towns grew rapidly from the mid-nineteenth century. Grandiose Victorian buildings were erected, and suburbs of gracious houses with large gardens were built. The first street trees were planted in these areas. At the same time, the working classes lived in a densely-built urban environment, often lacking the basic necessities for health and hygiene, let alone the benefit of urban green spaces and the amenity of the Georgian park. Perhaps, as a result of the speed with which the Victorian town developed, and the enormous difference between the environment of the rich and that of the poor, the need for social reform rapidly became clear. A civic consciousness, which had always existed to some extent in towns, became an important motivation for change. It was recognised that amenity in towns was a broader concept than public-health issues, and included the presence of green spaces and parks for public use. This was made evident in 1840, when the Parliamentary Select Committee on the Health of Towns made recommendations not only for better housing and sanitation but also for 'public walks and open spaces'. A subsequent Act in 1843 made public money available for, amongst other things, the creation of urban parks.

Victorian parks were often the product of a cautious philanthropy, although, once created, they were handed over to the local authority for management. They tended, however, to be located in the more middle-class areas of the town. For example, although public funds were provided under the 1843 legislation for Paxton's Birkenhead Park in Liverpool, it was designed to be surrounded by speculatively-built villas for the wealthier classes, who would thereby pay for, and gain the advantage of, living close to the park. The formal design of parks of this period, their location and the strict regulations imposed on users by the municipal parks authorities, were a reflection of the society by which they were created. But the important principle had been established, that the amenity of green spaces was an essential part of the urban structure, and its upkeep a municipal responsibility. It did not, however, extend to the town as a whole, and there were relatively few urban parks.

THE GARDEN CITY MOVEMENT

During the later Victorian period, the garden city movement grew out of a desire to improve the urban environment, particularly that of the poor. Patrick Geddes[2] had, in 1904, described a process of city development which would commence with the planning of parks and gardens. Ebenezer Howard's concept of the garden city[3], however, was more practical, and saw urban green space both as a visual amenity and as productive land. The population of the garden city would farm the green space for food, as well as benefit from the proximity of the countryside. The green spaces upon which the garden city was based would be a civic responsibility, owned and maintained by the residents as an essential element of the urban fabric. In contrast to the Victorian park, where the provision of urban green space was a philanthropic gesture towards the provision of amenity, in the garden city, access to green space was the fundamental right of every citizen. It was from these developing attitudes to green space in towns that a deeper understanding grew during the early years of the twentieth century. It became generally accepted that the quality of life resided both in the provision of physical comforts and in the right of access to green spaces and amenity. Moreover, it became a widely-held view that access to amenity was the prerogative of the whole community.

THE CONCEPT OF URBAN AMENITY

At the same time as this consciousness was developing, large areas of the countryside around towns were being destroyed or sterilised by ribbon development and unplanned speculative house-building, which spread as a result of cheap public transport. The realisation that it was necessary to protect the countryside near towns, and to guide development so as to ensure the protection of amenity, led to the Ribbon Development Acts, Green Belt legislation, and the various Town Planning Acts of the 1920s and '30s. Public acceptance that state intervention through planning was necessary to preserve amenity for the benefit of the whole community was a significant extension of the civic consciousness of the Victorians. The basis for these changing attitudes may be found in the enormously influential book, *Britain and the beast*, edited by Clough Williams Ellis, in 1937.[4] It did much to identify the pressures which were destroying the quality of the urban environment, and defined the concept of amenity as a public concern which could only be protected by state action. It galvanised influential public interest and support for the development of the protective Town and Country Planning system.

Urban amenity was given further impetus by the need to

rebuild after the war. The influential Barlow Report of 1940,[5] which examined the distribution and living conditions of the industrial population, recognised that improving the quality of the environment in the older industrial areas was of prime importance as a precursor to attracting new industry. The report recommended state aid to reclaim derelict land, improve the industrial environment and induce industry to relocate where it was most needed. The Reith Committee[6] in 1956 saw the creation of the new town, with its framework of green spaces, as an essential element in future urban development, and its provision as a state responsibility. A further report by the Hobhouse Committee in 1947,[7] led to the establishment of the National Parks, thus spreading the idea of the park and of amenity far beyond the Victorian concept. Taken together, these proposals represented an enormous widening of the principle of state responsibility for the environment, and a broadening of the concept of amenity to include reinstatement of derelict land as a public responsibility, as well as the provision of more green spaces. The impetus which was to translate the reports into working legislation was provided by the surprise Labour victory in the general election of 1945. Access to amenity, both locally and at the national level became, in this way, a national right.

MODERN NEW TOWNS

From 1946 to 1950, fourteen New Towns were designated around London to rehouse the excess population from the capital. Between 1950 and 1961, only Cumbernauld, which absorbed overspill population from the slum clearance areas of Glasgow was designated then, from 1961 to 1970, a further fourteen New Towns were designated in various parts of the country. As a common feature, each New Town had an extraordinarily high proportion of green space for each inhabitant, compared with many existing towns. Green space was, however, designed as a public amenity and the private garden, important to Howard as a source of food production, was reduced in importance. The town plans were examples of how green spaces can become central features which penetrate and link the whole of the urban area, providing definition and giving identity to different parts of the town, with immediate access to the amenity for the whole population (Plates **49, 50**). It is important to note that this principle was extended and developed in the New Towns where experiments with total vehicle/pedestrian separation became common, notably the 'Radburn' housing layouts which gave vehicles access from one side of the housing cluster and pedestrians access from the other.

ENVIRONMENTAL IMPROVEMENT IN OLDER TOWNS

The New Town is a totally planned environment which is generally built on a green field site, using a simplified local administration. Older towns face much more complex problems and, during the mid-1970s, the problems of the environment of the Inner City became the focus of attention, areas of intense social, environmental and economic deprivation at the centre of the larger old industrial cities of Britain. New Towns seemed to emphasise the difference all the more strongly. The inner city was deprived of industry, deserted by the more able proportion of its population, partly crowded with substandard housing, and partly laid waste by slum clearance and the building of urban motorways. In the mid-1970s, there was a two-fold reaction to this – a strong government policy movement away from the New Towns which, it was held, had fulfilled their purpose, and a movement of resources into the inner cities. A major aspect of this policy was to improve the environment of the inner city through strategies such as the General Improvement Area (GIA) and the Housing Action Area (HAA). Essentially, these were aimed at upgrading substandard housing, introducing tree-planting to make streets more pleasant, and landscaping available green spaces as a way of improving the environment rapidly.

The General Improvement Area was created by the 1969 Housing Act, as a reaction from earlier concepts of comprehensive redevelopment. Its purpose was to concentrate environmental improvement on areas of towns rather than individual householders since 'The effort and resources devoted to improvement provide a much better return when directed to the upgrading of whole areas – the houses and the environment'.[8] In the ten years since the Act, over 1000 neighbourhoods containing over 30,000 houses have publicly financed environmental improvement work, and private house improvement was found to be only partially successful and has been largely superseded by other improvement strategies. The cost of environmental improvements, for instance, such as off-street parking, cosmetic improvements and landscaped playgrounds, has varied greatly between

£50 to over £1000, depending on the attitude of the local authority. It has been argued that the philosophy behind the GIA – to improve the environment with the expectation that landlords and householders will follow by improving their own properties with grant aid – was too optimistic and that the biggest incentive to householders to carry out improvements is the level of grant aid. However, the GIA programme has been successful in introducing more landscaping and street trees into those areas most in need of green space.

The Housing Act of 1974 developed the principles of urban renewal along the lines of the GIA but through the Housing Action Area (HAA), which provided more direct cash grants to landlords and householders and, in general, less for external environmental improvements. Attention was drawn in the legislation to gradual renewal and the potential of a corporate approach to the improvement of neighbourhood environments was laid more firmly on the local authority. Under HAA legislation, the extent of landscaping and environmental improvement depended on the priorities of the Local Authority and was subject to fluctuations in the rate support grant. A reduction in the rate support grant had the effect of encouraging local authorities to reduce further the extent of landscaping and other environmental improvement measures. In consequence, the HAA has been less effective than the GIA as a means of providing urban landscaping but, in certain areas, has been successful.

The principle has been extended to some of the older industrial areas, such as Rochdale, Lancashire, and Glasgow. There, it is intended to improve the amenity of the environment for the benefit of existing workers and to attract new industries. In each case, one of the key elements is landscaping – further expansion of the concept of public amenity. Green spaces and trees are planted in order to screen unpleasant areas quickly, create a sense of locality and improve living conditions. The provision of this green space is fundamentally different from the earlier amenity of Victorian parks, firstly, in its small scale; secondly, in its concern to improve the worst parts of the environment of the city; and thirdly, because it is totally a public responsibility.

PLANNING CONTROLS AND AMENITY

The examples quoted above illustrate attempts to introduce

green spaces into old and new towns, principally through the action of the state. However, just as town planners plan towns without actually owning them, through the application of development controls and various incentives available to developers, so planning the landscape of towns in a similar way has become accepted practice (Plates **51, 52**). It is becoming increasingly rare for all but the smallest developments to be granted planning permission without conditions specifying landscape treatment. Such landscaping conditions vary between the simple requirement that street trees be planted at the developer's expense, to more far-reaching agreements under Section 52 of the 1971 Town and Country Planning Act, which regulate the use of extensive areas of land and landscape. The intention is either to modify the impact of new development, to replace street trees that have been lost or to retain valuable features in a landscape which is undergoing development. In large schemes, the provisions for landscaping can be far-reaching and complex. An example of this may be seen at Ingleby Barwick, near Middlesbrough, where an estate of 15,000 houses planned in six villages has been proposed by private developers (figure **6.1**).

In total, the area of land to be developed is 716 ha, of which 353 is proposed for housing. Apart from internal open spaces and road corridors, there is 193 ha of peripheral land, principally along the steep river banks of the Tees and the Leven. 14.3 ha of this land is owned by the developers who, as a condition of being granted outline planning permission, entered into a Section 52 agreement in order to maintain the existing landscape character of that part of the valleys. The remaining areas are in multiple ownership and, where possible, the local authority is seeking to extend the Section 52 agreements to other landowners, with the long-term objective of creating a riverside park. The builders of each individual village will, similarly, be expected to carry out intensive landscaping work, with the intention of creating a high-quality new urban environment. Before the landscape masterplan for the project was drawn up, a survey was made of all hedgerows, mature trees and streams, as a base for the proposed landscape infrastructure. The initial landscape survey also identified sites for ponds which would eventually become features in the mature landscape, as well as balancing ponds to control the flow of storm water. On completion, the landscape will be handed over to the local authority for maintenance.

A similar philosophy underlines the introduction of design

135

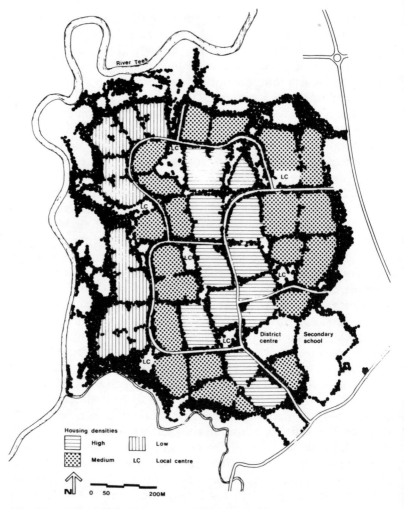

Housing densities

High

Low

Medium

LC   Local centre

N   0   50   200M

Fig. 6.1.   Ingleby Barwick landscape master plan

guidance for prospective developers. Here, the local authority
identifies aspects of the local environment which developers
should take into account in their proposals, in order to increase
their chances of being granted planning permission. Landscape
features prominently in the design guides that have been
produced to date. An excellent example of such a design guide
(figures **6.2, 6.3**), and one of the earliest, is that produced by
Essex County Council[9]. In over 130 pages, it sets out the

136

county's development control policy for residential areas, and develops physical and visual criteria for assessing the merit of proposed schemes through a series of case studies. Principles of spatial design are illustrated using examples of urban and rural street scenes, and the guides also illustrate carefully how trees on heavily-wooded sites may be retained in the development, in order to contain the space around housing and define public and private zones. These design principles are extended in the *Essex Design Guide* to give lists of tree and shrub species suitable for planting, either as hedges, ground cover or avenue trees. Case studies could be collected to show how existing trees and new planting might be incorporated into a landscape-dominated housing estate. Such guides have no legal power to compel developers to adopt the principles put forward. However, they do state clearly the local authority's policy, against which applications are judged, and illustrate alternative solutions to housing and estate design. In terms of the landscape, they draw attention to the benefits of tree-planting – a factor often overlooked or treated superficially by developers – and allow the local authority to define its own approach to trees in new developments.

For many years, some developers have recognised that landscaping an estate greatly increases the value of houses at relatively low cost. This mainly applies to higher-priced developments, a good example of which is the estate at Goldsworth Park, Surrey, a prizewinning design which included lakeside housing, amenity areas and extensive landscaping. See figure **6.4**.

Another example is New Ash Green, a new village built by speculative developers in the green belt in Kent. Since, in its design and architecture, New Ash Green is uncharacteristic of Kentish villages, existing woodlands were combined with extensive areas of landscaping in order to provide ' a thread of the Kent countryside running through the village . . .'. See figure **6.5**.

An important concept was that the developers encouraged the establishment of a village association and residents' societies to take over the management of the landscape. Income derived from membership fees for each body is used to pay for direct-labour landscape maintenance work, which is supplemented by the work of the association and the residents' societies themselves.

Total acreages of different landscapes, and the areas for which

Formal Arcadia

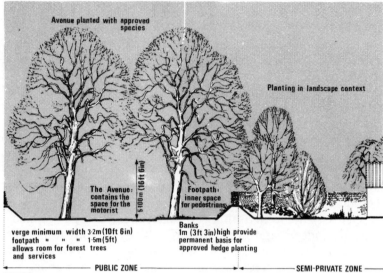

Avenue planted with approved species

Planting in landscape context

5·100m (16ft 6in)

The Avenue: contains the space for the motorist

Footpath: inner space for pedestrians

Banks 1m (3ft 3in) high provide permanent basis for approved hedge planting

verge minimum width 3·2m (10ft 6in)
footpath " " " 1·5m (5ft)
allows room for forest trees and services

— PUBLIC ZONE — SEMI-PRIVATE ZONE —

4.142 a Section

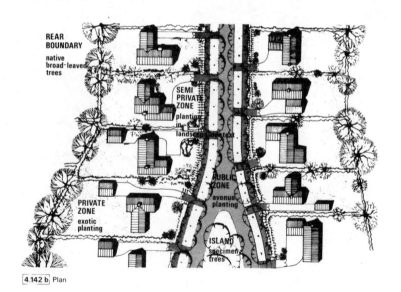

REAR BOUNDARY

native broad-leaved trees

SEMI PRIVATE ZONE

planting in landscape context

PUBLIC ZONE

avenue planting

PRIVATE ZONE

exotic planting

ISLAND specimen trees

4.142 b Plan

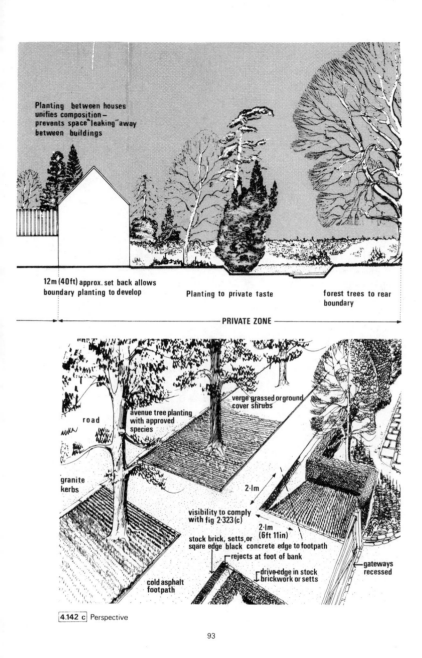

Planting between houses unifies composition – prevents space "leaking" away between buildings

12m (40ft) approx. set back allows boundary planting to develop

Planting to private taste

forest trees to rear boundary

PRIVATE ZONE

verge grassed or ground cover shrubs

avenue tree planting with approved species

road

granite kerbs

2·1m

visibility to comply with fig 2·323(c)

2·1m (6ft 11in)

stock brick, setts, or sqare edge black concrete edge to footpath

rejects at foot of bank

drive edge in stock brickwork or setts

gateways recessed

cold asphalt footpath

4.142 c Perspective

93

Fig. 6.2. Essex Design Guide: formal arcadia. Courtesy Essex County Council

139

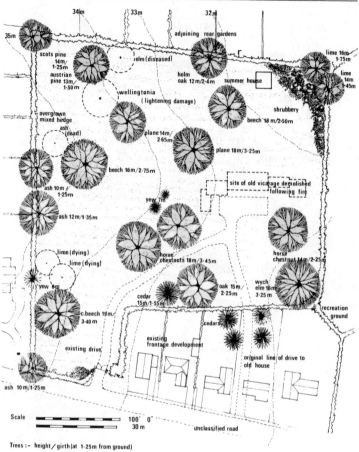

Trees :– height / girth (at 1·25m from ground)

Fig. 6.3. Essex Design Guide: low-density case study. Courtesy Essex County Council

This drawing shows:

1   Survey of existing trees, indicating height and spread, and girth, with those to be removed shown dotted. The remainder are worthy of a Tree Preservation Order.

2   Surrounding boundaries, adjoining development, existing access and levels.

3   Site of demolished buildings and large 'summer house' suitable for conversion to a garage.

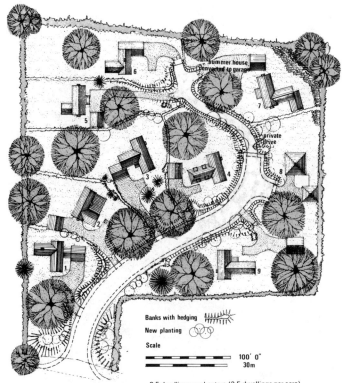

Banks with hedging

New planting

Scale

100' 0"
30m

8.5 dwellings per hectare (3.5 dwellings per acre)

NOTE: It would of course be possible to develop this site at a higher density than shown in 4 23, and still retain the trees. This would, however, involve the use of both urban and rural principles of spatial organisation. If, for example, houses 1, 2, 3 and 4 are linked together by further buildings, urbanism is immediately the dominant principle; the trees will modify the urban space.
trees).

1. PHYSICAL
(a) Utilises site efficiently—only 20% used for public zone, (access drives, screened and gated, are part of private zone).
(b) Privacy requirements met by design—in public zone buildings set back to allow screening by hedges, banks and trees. In private zone landscape or remoteness effectively prevent over-looking.
2. VISUAL
(a) Uses rural system of spatial organisation, landscape contains and dominates buildings.
(b) Existing trees are retained; their random grouping suggests informal arcadian solution.
(c) Winding road with dark surface combined with parking and garaging concealed in landscape reduces visual intrusion of the vehicle.
(d) New hedges, banks, and tree planting visually contain the public space.

Fig. 6.4. Goldsworth Park lakeside scheme incorporating housing clusters and landscaping. Photo: Brian Clouston and Partners and New Ideal and Willett Homes

different bodies are responsible, are given in tables 1, 2 and 4, and proposed maintenance tasks for the main land-use areas are given in table 3. These tables form part of the New Ash Green Landscape Report.[10] New Ash Green provides a very rare example of a new community assuming the direct responsibility for maintaining the landscape of the village in which they have

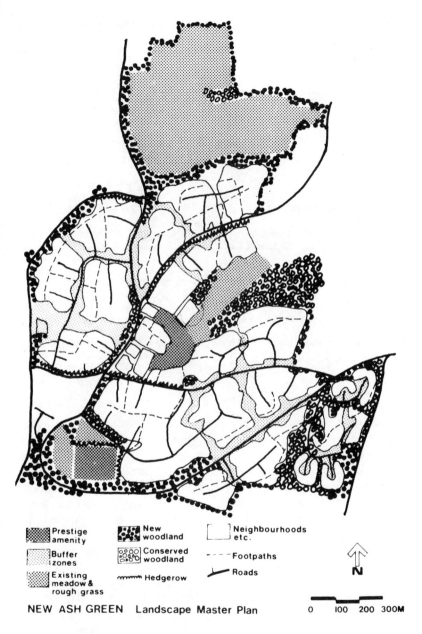

Prestige amenity

Buffer zones

Existing meadow & rough grass

New woodland

Conserved woodland

Hedgerow

Neighbourhoods etc.

Footpaths

Roads

N

NEW ASH GREEN Landscape Master Plan

0   100   200 300M

Fig. 6.5. New Ash Green landscape master plan. From NAG Report, Brian Clouston and Partners.

143

Table 6.1. Acreages and management responsibilities: New Ash Green

Area	Village association	Residents' societies	Total
1. Existing woodland retained	35.8		35.8
2. New woodland	22.0		22.0
3. Buffer zones between neighbourhoods	41.5		41.5
4. Grassland	28.4		28.4
5. Neighbourhood units		190.5	190.5
6. Miscellaneous infrastructure	31.3		31.3*
	159.0	190.5	349.5

* To the extent that the highway authority will take over various road maintenance responsibilities, this figure will be slightly reduced.

This table is extracted from New Ash Green Report, Brian Clouston and Partners.

chosen to live. It is unlikely to be a formula which will be widely acceptable in other urban areas which lack the homogeneity of the new village.

Taken as a whole, the planning controls which the local authority exert over the landscaping of new developents, and the GIA and HAA initiatives taken in existing urban areas, represent a relatively sophisticated approach to the landscaping of towns. In the first place, the assumption is made that society as a whole will benefit from the inclusion of landscaping with new developments. In the second place, an incentive is offered to the developer to provide landscaping in order to increase his chances of obtaining planning permission. In poorer neighbourhoods, such as those which become the subject of GIA's and HAA's, it is accepted that external improvements, such as landscaping and tree-planting, are important in creating the climate of optimism which encourages local residents and landlords to improve their property.

Table 6.2. Village association acreages: New Ash Green

Area	Present*	Eventual
Existing woodland retained		
Nine Horse Wood	17.6	17.6
Bazes Shaw	1.8	1.8
Redhill Wood	–	11.8
Springcroft Wood	–	0.6
Turner's Oak Shaw	1.0	1.0
Ash Road Wood	0.7	0.7
Northern agricultural wood	–	2.3
	21.1	35.8
New woodland	–	22.0
Buffer zones	5.2†	41.5
Grassland		
Playing field	7.2	7.2
The Minnis	3.3	3.3
Meadow	–	9.2
Sports ground		5.8
Orchard		2.9
	10.5	28.4
Miscellaneous		
Carparks	–	2.0
Manor House	–	2.8
Roads, paths, hedges, etc.	–	26.5
	–	31.3
Totals	36.8	159.0

* Village association at present manage on behalf of Bovis.
† Village association entirely responsible.

This table is extracted from New Ash Green Report, Brian Clouston and Partners.

Table 6.3. Use/management assumptions for main land areas: New Ash Green

Area	Assumed use	Level of maintenance/actions to be taken (H = high; M = medium; L = low)
Existing woodland		
Nine Horse Wood	Walking; riding; visual amenity; adventure areas for children; pillaging and dumping-ground for residents as development proceeds and children grow up (unless careful).	H in accessible areas: M in protected areas where coppice being converted to standards. Woodland fringes allowed to grow wild and form impenetrable barrier. During development, high level of care for trees to be retained.
Redhill and Bowes Woods	Buffer framework/visual screen for housing developments; walking; treehouse-style play areas; picnicking by adjacent residents; (motorized litter dump for residents unless careful).	H wherever access is free. In all woods, consideration should be given to the scope for zoning and rotating active and non-use areas. Protection of newly-planted areas and fringes. Access points and routes to be well defined.
Bazes Shaw Wood	Nature reserve and nature trail/study area for use by local naturalist society and, by children attending nearby school, as an outdoor laboratory.	Management based on conservation practices and geared to the demonstration of ecological principles of vegetational succession, etc. Work by naturalist society and school volunteers. Protection from residents moving to and from meadow essential: access points to the wood should be counter to popular demand.
New woodland		
Redhill and Bowes Woods	As above.	Protection until established. H in any areas which are subsequently accessible.
Western and northern belts	Wind break; visual screen/framework for future neighbourhoods.	L, after initial three years 'beating-up' and weed control.
Buffer zones	Increasing demand for informal 'let-off-steam' play areas. The 'thread of Kent countryside . . .'	L, apart from twice annual tree survey and occasional grass cutting. Once trees established, grass within the drifts might be mown 2-3 times annually. Alternatively, it can be left unmown.

Grassland

Cricket square	Progressively increased match use as surface becomes established; good sward	Relatively H, to provide for enjoyable village-class matches.
Outfield/soccer playing field	Increasing use for sports as population grows and good sward is established. (Planting of tree groups and gentle earth-contouring will give sense of enclosure.)	M, apart from *high* level of care in the case of worn areas, e.g. goal mouths. Rotational siting of pitches and goal areas.
Outer sports ground area	Area for tree-screen planting and scout camping. Fair/gymkhana/bonfire ground.	L.
The Minnis	Increasing use as the village green, once reasonable sward and a more inviting character are established.	M.
Nine Horse Meadow	Parkland for picnicking and walking/wild-flower collecting.	L, involving removal of grass mowings to increase botanical variety and interest of the sward.
Apple orchard	Apple trees retained but thinned to provide an attractive picnicking/playing area for local residents.	L.
Woodland grass fringes and rides	Walking, riding and nature study.	L, involving a twice-yearly mowing of *narrow* strip alongside paths.
Hedges	Increasing importance as visual screens and physical barriers.	H where gapping-up or replanting required: H where sight-lines involved and adjacent to houses. Other hedges require L or M according to whether or not they are in wilderness areas.
Neighbourhood units – communal space	An increasing range of active and passive uses as the population grows and its structure diversifies.	Generally, H throughout.
Prestige areas such as the Manor House, carparks and shopping centre		Generally, H throughout.

This table is extracted from New Ash Green Report, Brian Clouston and Partners.

Table 6.4.   Residents' societies' acreages: New Ash Green

A.   Gross neighbourhood areas

Existing/under construction

Punchcroft	11.7	Ayelands	10.5
Knightscroft	18.0	Chapel Wood	12.1
Overminnis	2.8	Penenden	8.9
Millfield	10.5	Farm Holt	18.5
Lambardes	7.6	Bazes Shaw	7.3*
Foxbury	2.1	Westfield	6.7
Coltstead	13.1	Manor Forstal	11.0
Capelands	11.7	Spring Cross	9.4
Sub-total	77.5	Bowes Wood	11.7
		Redhill Wood	13.4
		Old peoples' flats	2.1
		Sub-total	111.6

Total of all neighbourhood areas including 1.4 acres for children's play, 190.5 acres.

B.   Breakdown

	Millfield	Knightscroft	Capelands	Average
Area in acres	10.5	10.0†	11.7	10.7
Number of houses	169	117	91	126
Open space				
communal	5810††	5320††	5300)††	2.77
front garden areas	6510	7370	10000)	acres

* Reduced area.
† Phase 1 housing area.
†† Square yards.

This table is extracted from New Ash Green Report, Brian Clouston and Partners.

A TOWN LANDSCAPE MANAGEMENT PLAN

As a consequence of the uneven progress of urban development, and changes in public attitudes to amenity, there exists today a wide variety of green spaces in our urban areas. The maintenance of almost all of these areas has been accepted as the responsibility of the civic authorities, to be financed from the rates. In this context, the creation of a town landscape maintenance plan raises three main problems. Firstly, has the full potential of each green space been realised in terms of its benefit to the community? Secondly, are the resources spent on maintenance being used in the most cost-effective way? Thirdly, a tree takes a long time to mature and a policy of continuous replacement of street trees and shrubs should be planned many years in advance in order to avoid an empty appearance of familiar sites for long periods, as newly-planted trees replace mature specimens.

THE ROLE OF GREEN SPACES

There is an increasing demand for 'commons' and 'wilderness areas' in cities, as a contrast to the built urban environment, to protect flora and fauna and as a source of raw material for schoolchildren in outdoor study exercises. It has been questioned whether the formal park fulfils a valid role in towns today. Are carefully manicured green spaces the most appropriate environment for informal recreation and pop music festivals, or such activities as jogging, for example? The attitudes of those who will use the open space may differ from those of the local authority and the landscape architect responsible for creating and maintaining green spaces. Thus, it is important that the opinions of local people are taken into account, through consultation with local residents' associations or public participation exercises made under the requirements of the Town and Country Planning Acts.

Perhaps the largest area of green space in our cities consists of the neglected land, the canal banks and revegetated derelict land, which, at present, receives virtually no maintenance but which provides a potentially valuable resource. The variety of wildlife habitats is important ecologically and educationally, and this land is a valuable source of such habitats. Its characteristically linear form allows a network of interlinked greenery to be developed in our urban areas which is separate from the streets. A management plan would aim to improve access for recreational use while conserving the character of the resource, best achieved by a low-key maintenance programme.

One example of this is the 'greenway' concept (figure **6.6**) developed by one firm. Passenger railways are closely integrated with town centres and mineral lines with industrial sites, and these could all be developed as amenity corridors or greenways.

Fig. 6.6.   Greenway concept. Photo: Land Use Consultants

The easy gradients of existing derelict railway routes can be adapted to form a network of walkways, bridleways and cycleways, separate from traffic.

Where derelict land has been temporarily landscaped to improve the appearance of an area or to provide a suitable setting for future development, the type of planting is important. Simply grassing over the spaces, rather than giving them a positive use, can be a major drain on maintenance resources, as grass needs mowing three or four times a year and this is an expensive operation. They can be revegetated by using indigenous plants, which reduces maintenance costs and has the added advantage of being more attractive to wildlife.

The landscape management policy should include marginal land on the edges of the built-up area, sometimes cultivated, often neglected, awaiting development. Existing trees or hedgerows can, thereby, be preserved and the appearance of the marginal landscape improved. A semi-mature landscape, with trees of a wide age-range, can thus be produced, which will avoid the eventual problems of massive tree replacement we face now, at the same time forming an attractive setting for any development which might take place or a cleaner, more beautiful, edge to the town. Several attempts have been made to create and conserve such landscapes by agreement and incentives before development begins. The advance landscaping carried out in the Middlesbrough scheme, for instance, was based on careful conservation of existing trees and hedgerows.

Financial implications of maintaining green spaces
Finance devoted to green-space maintenance is closely linked to rate revenue and, consequently, tightly controlled. The replacement of street trees is a major expense, in view of the large number of over-mature trees in our towns. When, as in the case of Dutch elm disease, the loss of mature trees is sudden, the visual effect can be catastrophic, especially where elm was the dominant tree, as in Bristol which, since the 1960s, has lost some 2000 elms. The average cost of felling and clearing was £65 per tree. Other cities have been, or are likely to be, affected: Merseyside County Council has spent £50,000 on 'sanitation felling'. Greater Manchester Council, fearing the spread of the disease could eventually cost £3 million for treatment, instigated a five-year emergency treatment scheme at a cost of £80,000. In Edinburgh, there are some 25,000 elms, most of them in the 'New Town' and Princes Street garden, where they are key elements in the street scene and vulnerable to the disease, which has already reached the area. Elm disease is a particular phenomenon which has highlighted the importance of street trees and their vulnerability. However, the effects of potential future loss of aged street trees could be mitigated, and the costs spread more evenly, by a continuous policy of replanting and the diversification of tree species.

Maintenance costs in formal municipal parks are relatively high compared to the maintenance costs for street trees and

Table 6.5.   Landscape maintenance: Peterlee New Town

Land use breakdown	Acres	Hectares	Ratio L/scape area to development*			Cost per ha. (1978) to maintain (£ per year)
Residential	639 approx	257	1	2	3	
Howletch I	25	10	20	20	50	2500
Howletch II	34	14	20	20	50	2500
South West V	44.5	18	30	25	45	3000
South West V Private	12	5	15	35	50	3000
Lorimers Close	10	4	10	60	30	2000
Shotton Village	5	2	–	–	–	
Spire Hollin	12	5	–	–	–	
Eastdene	29	11	–	–	–	
Sunny Blunts	17.5	7	25	25	50	3000
Industry (gross)						
N.E. area	78	31	40	60		1500
N.W. area (Phase 1)	104	42	50	50		2000
N.W. area (Phase 2)	313	126	50	50		2000
Shopping area						
Town centre	26	10	25	75		3000
Neighbourhoods	9	3				
Public open space (approx)	260	105	....			2000
Private open space	7	3				
Playing fields	170	68				
Schools (approx)	150	61				
Woodland	617	250	....			500

Total 1.122 hectares

* 1 Landscape infrastructure.
2 Public open space and parkland.
3 Residential area.

'common lands'. Mowing costs are high, as are costs for maintaining ornamental shrubs, replacing bedding plants, and providing fertilizer and weed-killer. Also, the seasonal nature of park upkeep makes it difficult to balance work and labour availability throughout the year. This is especially true in local authorities which have a high proportion of formal parks. As long ago as 1956, Sylvia Crowe[11] pointed out that maintenance costs per year on Wimbledon Common were less than 3 per cent of those of Kensington Gardens.

New town landscapes are cheaper to maintain than formal parks since, in general, landscaped areas are treated in a less ornamental fashion. In addition, the large scale of new-town landscaping leads to economies in maintenance costs. However, overall maintenance per hectare may vary from £500 per hectare per year for woodlands to £3,000 per hectare per year for residential areas. A typical analysis of landscape maintenance costs for areas of Peterlee New Town in County Durham is given in table 5.

As a whole, new-town green spaces are more 'balanced' in seasonal demnd for labour, since they generally contain a variety of landscape types ranging from forestry to high-maintenance parks. A principal question facing the New Town, as it nears completion and handover to local authorities, is the large demand for trained maintenance labour. Often, the local authorities involved have little experience of the range and scale of maintenance costs. New Ash Green offers a different perspective on landscape management in housing areas. There, the landscape forms a dominant element in the overall environment, as shown in land-use terms in table 1 (see p.144). Actual landscape management is a labour-intensive operation in many areas of the village and work is divided between the village association and residents societies, and a direct labour force under the control of a landscape manager. An outline of annual landscape management tasks is given in table 3, (see p.147), and costs are shown in table 6.

This does not include any notional cost for the time donated voluntarily by members of the village. Association estimates have been made of the proportion of income arising from the membership fees of the residents' bodies which may be allocated to landscape maintenance. These are given in table 6.

The type of maintenance skill required in landscaped urban renewal schemes, such as GIA differs from the traditional horticultural skills needed in formal parks. Maintenance, in this sense, frequently involves minor house repairs and clearing-out of dustbin stores, as well as weeding shrub beds and removing litter. Often, it is more successfully carried out by one man in a local area, rather than being treated as part of the maintenance work of a city department.

Data on the maintenance costs for landscaping in older urban areas is very difficult to assemble, partly because the responsibility for its upkeep often varies between several agencies, and partly because the green spaces themselves vary so much. It is common to find maintenance of Victorian cemeteries adjacent to recent landscaping carried out under GIA legisla-

Table 6.6. Estimated annual maintenance costs: New Ash Green

	Village association	Residents' societies	Total
Total acreages involved	156.2	49	205.2
Manpower			
Estates manager*	800	1200	2000
Foreman	1000	1500	2500
Three permanent staff	2160	3240	5400
Six temporary staff	1800	3600	5400
Sub-total	5760	9540	15300
Machinery			
Depreciation (20% p.a.)	600	600	1200
Maintenance/repairs	600	600	1200
Sub-total	1200	1200	2400
Materials			
Fuel, fertilizers, sprays, fencing, gravel, replacements† stakes, etc.	1500	2500	4000
Administration/overheads	1000	1000	2000
Totals	9460	14240	23700
Cost per acre	60	290	115

* Estates manager should oversee all works on behalf of village association and residents' societies and 50% only of his time would be available for landscape management work. This time should then be apportioned, as also with his staff, va 40%: rs 60%.
† 2% p.a. @ £1 sq.yd. for plants. (This item alone accounts for £1640.)

This table is extracted from New Ash Green Report, Brian Clouston and Partners.

tion. In view of the enormous scale of environmental improvement, especially in terms of improving the landscape, which is being carried out in Glasgow, detailed assessments have been

Table 6.7. Income from membership fees for landscape maintenance: New Ash Green.

Income/expenses	Village association	Residents' societies	Totals
Probable net income (landscape purse)	9,600	18,000	17,600
Total annual costs	9,460	14,240	23,700
Surplus	140	3,760	3,900

This table is extracted from New Ash Green Report, Brian Clouston and Partners.

made of the maintenance requirements of landscape areas. This was undertaken as part of a more detailed study called the *Glasgow Eastern Area Renewal Project* (GEAR), discussed in more detail below.

To arrive at cost estimates, urban landscape areas were assessed in terms of the ratio of open to planted areas. An estimate was then made of the need for machine and manual labour, and an overall estimate of maintenance costs for each type of area. These are shown in table 8. The results show a very wide variation in maintenance costs from low-maintenance grass-only areas which are found to require between £700 and £840 per hectare per year for maintenance, to high-maintenance areas with a 2:1 ratio of grass to shrubs, which require up to £8,000 per hectare per year.

The variety of green spaces, both old and new, in towns, makes the task of defining a town-landscaping management plan extremely difficult. To be complete, such a plan would have to include green spaces in the inner city, the suburbs and the outer fringes of towns, where farming comes into conflict with expanding town boundaries. It would include the range of agencies involved in maintenance, the policies of planning authorities and the financial demands such maintenance would make on rate revenue.

Glasgow Eastern Area Renewal Project

In a number of ways, the most comprehensive attempt at such a plan has been the GEAR project[12]. Because of the very large

Table 6.8. Machine and manual maintenance costs: GEAR

Ratio of grass to planting	Level of maintenance	Manual ops + 35% Overhead m/hr	£	Machine ops + 40% Overhead m/hr	£	Total m/hr per 1000m² m/hr	£	Total manual cost per ha. £000/ha	Total men per ha* Men/ha	Cost of material £	Machinery and equip Fixed costs. £	Machinery Variable costs £	Total cost per ha £000
2:1	H	152–186	360–440	104–128	245–300	256–314	605–740	6.1–7.4	1.2–1.5	210–250	310–390	70–80	6.7 – 8.1
	M	40–50	95–120	94–114	220–270	134–164	315–390	3.1–3.9	0.6–.78	140–180	290–350	65–75	3.6 – 4.5
	L	22–26	50–60	3.4–4.2	8–10	25.4–30.2	58–70	.6–.7	.12–.14	80–100	50–70	4–6	.73 – .88
4:1	H	108–130	255–310	109–133	260–315	217–266	515–625	5.1–6.2	1.04–1.27	150–190	330–410	75–85	5.7 – 6.9
	M	34–42	80–100	96–116	225–275	130–158	305–375	3.1–3.7	.62–.76	120–140	290–350	65–75	3.6 – 4.3
	L	22–26	50–60	4.2–5.0	10–12	26.2–31.0	60–.72	.6–.7	.12–.14	60–80	50–70	4–6	.71 – .85
6:1	H	93–113	220–270	110–134	260–315	203–247	460–585	4.6–5.8	.97–1.18	140–180	330–410	75–85	5.1 – 6.5
	M	33–41	80–100	97–117	230–280	130–158	310–380	3.1–3.8	.62–.76	110–130	290–350	65–75	3.6 – 4.4
	L	22–26	50–60	4.4–5.2	9–12	26.4–31.2	59–72	.6–.7	.12–.14	60–80	50–70	4–6	.71 – .85

8:1	H	77–83	180–200–	111–135	265–320	188–218	445–520	4.4–5.2	.9–1.1	120–140	330–410	75–85	4.9 – 5.8
	M	31–39	75–90	97–117	230–280	128–156	305–370	3.1–3.7	.62–.76	100–120	290–350	65–75	3.5 – 4.2
	L	22–26	50–60	4.7–5.7	11–13	26.7–31.7	61–73	.6–.7	.12–.14	50–70	50–70	4–6	.70 – .84
10:1	H	.70–84	165–200	112–136	265–320	182–240	430–520	4.3–5.2	.87–1.1	110–130	330–410	75–85	4.8 – 5.8
	M	31–37	75–90	98–118	230–280	129–185	305–370	3.1–3.7	.62–.76	100–120	290–350	65–75–	3.5 – 4.2
	L	22–26	50–60	4.7–5.7	11–13	26.7–31.7	61–73	.6–.7	.12–.14	50–70	50–70	4–6	.70 – .84
12:1	H	63–77	150–180	113–137	270–325	176–214	420–505	4.2–5.1	.85–1.0	110–130	330–410	75–85	4.7 – 5.7
	M	30–36	70–85	98–118	230–280	128–154	300–365	3.0–3.6	.61–.74	100–120	290–350	65–75	3.4 – 4.1
	L	22–26	50–60	4.7–5.3	11–13	26.7–31.3	61–73	.6–.7	.12–.14	50–70	50–70	4–6	.70 – .84
Grass only + trees	H	39–47	90–110	114–147	270–325	153–183	360–435	3.6–4.3	.74–.88	90–110	330–410	70–85	4.1 – 4.9
	M	28–33	65–80	97–120	230–285	115–154	295–365	2.95–3.65	.55–0.74	85–105	290–350	65–75	3.4 – 4.1
	L	22–26	50–60	5.2–6.2	10–15	27.2–32.2	60–75	0.6–0.75	0.13–0.15	45–55	50–70	4–6	.7 – .84

Notes. The workload between summer and winter operations tends to be in favour of summer operations. The figures given above take no account of such fluctuations, as they provide broad indications of manpower for long-term budgeting only.

Annual maintenance cost estimates related to variable proportions of grass to border planting in high, medium and low maintenance sites.

This table is extracted from GEAR Report, Brian Clouston and Partners and Cobham Resource Consultants.

financial commitment to environmental improvement in Glasgow made by the Scottish Development Agency, the City of Glasgow Council and Strathclyde Regional Council, it was decided to draw up guide-lines to relate landscape designs to management. This was to ensure the most cost-effective environmental renewal, to allow municipal funds to be allocated correctly and to ensure that enough resources were allocated to maintenance at the time when the landscape scheme was concerned. The document is a landscape management plan which concentrates on the inner city rather than the other, less pressing, problems of the urban fringe, giving landscape guidance for new developers.

The GEAR manual is intended to achieve the fullest possible integration between the landscape design concept and its maintenance implications. As a preliminary, a survey was made of existing environmental conditions affecting landscaping in the east end of Glasgow. Fifteen different types of landscaped area were identified in the region. These ranged from the landscaping around tower blocks to burial grounds. Thirty-nine sites were surveyed, in order to gauge the existing landscape components, current maintenance was assessed, and notes made on the relationship between design, use and maintenance. The results of this survey are summarised in table 9.

Following this, a study was carried out of the available maintenance agencies to determine which was most suitable for each type of landscape maintenance. The study explored the capabilities of organisations, both public and private, official and voluntary, and assessed the experience of other agencies in employing maintenance contractors. Agencies included in the study were: Glasgow Parks Department, other local government departments, public agencies such as the Property Services Agency, private contractors, voluntary labour and community groups.

A referencing system was proposed, in view of the wide range of design teams involved, both public and private, and the variety of contractors concerned with landscape design and maintenance. The system obliges the designer to estimate maintenance needs as design work proceeds, and enables the landscape manager to assess the implications of plans in terms of manpower and equipment.

Essentially, information on each landscaping project is collected, covering the expected life of the site, the basic land-

158

Table 6.9. Survey of existing environmental conditions: GEAR

Land-use categories	Broad landscape functions	Present standard of maintenance	Desirable/assumed level of maintenance	Survey components – general
Industry	F.S. V.A.	Medium	M – L	A lack of green space.
Residential				
Tenement blocks	A.R.i. P.R. V.A. F.S.	Low – very low	M – H	Poor facilities and neglect resulting in variable level of appearance.
Estates of detached and semi detached houses	A.R.i. P.R. V.A. F.S.	Medium – low	M – H	Cluttered landscapes result in difficulty in maintenance and consequent neglect.
Tower blocks	A.R.i. P.R. V.A. F.S.	Medium – low	M – H	Parkland settings reasonably maintained, otherwise lack of maintenance especially with borders. High-use pressure.
Open space in curtilage of public buildings				
Specific				
Educational – schools etc.	A.R.f. A.R.i. P.R. F.S. V.A.	Medium	H – M	Borders and planting poorly maintained. Grass and hard surface generally adequate.
Hospitals	F.S. V.A.	High – medium	M – L	Generally well-maintained.
Various				
Libraries/local government etc. police, sewage etc.	F.S. V.A.	High – medium	M – L	A lack of green space.
Recreation				
Open space, large parks	A.R.f. A.R.i. P.R. V.A. F.S.	High – medium	H – M – L	Maintained to the highest standard observed in the survey.
Open space, small parks	A.R.i. P.R. V.A. F.S.	Medium – poor	M – L	General neglect when compared with larger parks.
Open space sports facilities – bowls, golf, playing fields	A.R.f. A.R.i. V.A.	High – medium	H – M	Generally high standard, user pressure shown by wear in places.
Gap sites (Temporary land-use)	F.S. +/– V.A.	Low – very low	H – M – L	Not maintained, generally unmaintainable.

Key to landscape functions: A.R.f. Active recreation – formal, A.R.i. Active recreation – informal, P.R. Passive recreation, V.A. Visual amenity, F.S. Functional services – these cover such items as the provision of access and the provision/accommodation of those non-recreational activities/services normally associated with the landscape category in question.

This table is extracted from GEAR Report, Brian Clouston and Partners and Cobham Resource Consultants

159

Table 6.10. Design/maintenance system for planting: GEAR

Ref.	Code	Landscape Components	Maintenance level – high — Site life 10Yrs+Perm	5 – 10Yrs Inter	–5Yrs Temp	Maintenance level – medium — Site life 10Yrs+Prem
A		Grass areas				
	1	High quality – all grass mix with ryegrass.	*	*	*	*
	2	High quality alternative mis without ryegrass	*	*	*	*
	3	(Hydroseed) – grass with clover mix	–	–	*	–
	4	Clover mix (only as underplant)	*	*	–	*
	5	Turf planting	*	*	*	*
B		Planted areas — Trees				
	1	Semi Mature	*	–	–	–
	2	Heavy nursery stock	*	–	–	–
	3	Tall standard	*	*	–	*
	4	Standard	*	*	*	*
	5	Feather	*	*	*	*
	6	Whip	*	*	–	*
	7	Transplant	–	*	–	–
C		Shrubs and climbers				
	1	Specimen	*	*	*	*
	2	Structure planting 2m +	*	*	*	*
	3	Mass planting 2m –	*	*	*	*
	4	Ornamental planting	*	*	*	*
	5	Climbers – self supporting	*	*	*	*
	6	Trellis/wire-mounted	*	–	–	–
D		Herbaceous				
	1	Mass planting	*	*	*	*
	2	Ornamental planting	*	*	–	–
E		Bedding plants	*	*	*	–
F		Bulbs/corms (naturalised)				
	1	In grass	*	*	*	*
	2	In border	*	*	*	*
G		Hedging				
	1	Vigorous	*	*	–	–
	2	Slow growing	*	–	–	*
H		Plants in portable containers	*	*	*	–

* Component may be used in design.
– Component may not be used in design.

160

5 – 10Yrs Inter	–5Yrs Temp	Maintenance level – low / Site life / 10Yrs+Prem	5 – 10Yrs Inter	–5Yrs Temp	Comments
*	*	*	*	–	
*	*	*	*	–	
*	*	–	*	*	
–	–	–	–	–	
*	–	*	–	–	
–	–	–	–	–	
–	–	–	–	–	
*	–	*	–	–	
*	*	*	–	–	
*	*	*	*	–	
*	–	*	*	–	
*	*	*	*	*	
*	*	*	*	*	Feature in grass
*	*	*	*	*	
*	–	*	–	–	Selection primaries for ornament.
*	–	*	–	–	
–	–	–	–	–	
*	*	*	*	*	Ground cover type
–	–	–	–	–	Trad. herbaceous
–	–	–	–	–	Includes bedding bulbs
*	*	*	*	*	
*	*	*	*	*	Naturalised
–	–	–	–	–	
–	–	–	–	–	
–	–	–	–	–	

This table is extracted from GEAR Report, Brian Clouston and Partners and Cobham Resources scape components (selected from a list of 26) and the required level of maintenance (high, medium or low). Maintenance requirements for each landscape component are set out in table 9.

An example of the maintenance referencing code, which brings together the information collected for each project, is given in table 10. Finally, a data sheet is prepared by measuring each landscape component involved, in order to obtain an estimate of total maintenance input and cost.

MAINTENANCE REFERENCING CODE

SITE LIFE				
ref.code \ maint.L		HIGH	MEDIUM	LOW
A 1	m^2			
2	m^2			
3	m^2			
5	m^2			
TOTAL				
A 4	m^2			
B 1	no			
2	no			
3	no			
4	no			
5	no			
6	no			
7	no			
TOTAL				
C 1	no			
2	m^2			
3	m^2			
4	m^2			
5	m^2			
6	m^2			
TOTAL excl C1				
D 1	m^2			
2	m^2			
TOTAL				
E 1	m^2			
F 1	m^2			
2	m^2			
TOTAL				
G 1	m_{lin}			
2	m_{lin}			
TOTAL				
H 1	m^2			
grass edges	m_{lin}			
obstruction	no			
hard surface	m			
path edges	m_{lin}			
channels	m_{lin}			

162

The GEAR manual goes on to discuss the optimum size of contract which should be let at each stage of renewal. This allows an estimate to be made of staff requirements and the level of responsibility to be assumed by each landscape manager or maintenance team. Similarly, the question of the contract agreement most suitable for inner-city landscape work is discussed. Finally, recommendations are made on the present three-year landscaping handover period, and the implications of an extended four-year period.

CONCLUSION

There have been many changes in the types of green space incorporated in urban areas, and profound changes in public attitudes towards their use and value. Generally, the local authority is now responsible for the maintenance and upkeep of these green spaces. Over the past twenty years, changes have taken place rapidly and a wide variety of green spaces has been provided through environmental improvement work, new towns, the applications of planning conditions and the provision of design guidance. To maintain these areas, while at the same time conserving the Victorian legacy of formal parks, is likely to be a major burden on local authorities. Just as public attitudes to amenity change, the use made of the town's structure of green spaces is not static. It is necessary, therefore, to analyse the types of green space in the town and to consider their uses in relation to developing needs. Thus, the problems of allocating resources for maintenance may be considered more clearly and a sensible programme, which recognises the need for continuous renewal and maintenance, put forward.

Over the past twenty years, more trees have been planted in towns for amenity reasons than ever before. More types of green space have been, and are being, created through legislation and public action. At present, the greatest part of this landscaping is relatively new. Street trees planted in the 1960s will not reach maturity until 2060 but, in the meantime, it is necessary to recognise that, as these mature, our existing stock of trees and green spaces will be reaching senility. It is essential, therefore, that we take stock of our urban green spaces, understand their contribution to the amenity of towns, and their vulnerability, and design our landscape management plans accordingly.

REFERENCES

1 W.G. Hoskins, *The making of the English landscape,* London, Hodder and Stoughton, 1955
2 P. Geddes, *Cities in evolution,* London, Williams and Northgate, 1915
3 E. Howard, *Garden cities of tomorrow,* London, Faber, 1946. Originally published in 1898 as *Tomorrow: a peaceful path the real reform*
4 C. Williams Ellis (ed), *Britain and the beast, London, Dent, 1937*
5 *Report of the Royal Commission on the Distribution of the Industrial Population,* London, HMSO, 1940, Cmnd 6153
6 Lord Reith, *Second report of the Committee on New Towns,* London, HMSO, 1946
7 *Report on national parks administration,* London, HMSO, 1947
8 MHLG Circular 65/69 (WO 64/69), Housing Act 1969, Area Improvement, para 3
9 Essex County Council, *A design guide for residential areas,* Chelmsford, 1973
10 J.B. Clouston and Partners, New Ash Green landscape report, 1972 (unpublished)
11 S. Crowe, *Tomorrow's landscape, London, Faber, 1956*
12 J.B. Clouston and Partners and Cobham Resources, *Glasgow Eastern Area renewal project,* Scottish Development Agency, 1978

Index

References to plate illustrations are in italics

166

168